Utility-S[tyle]

QUILTS FOR EVERYDAY LIVING

sharon holland

Utility-Style
Quilts for Everyday Living
Copyright © 2017 by Landauer Publishing, LLC
Projects Copyright © 2017
by Sharon Holland

This book was designed, produced,
and published by
Landauer Publishing, LLC
3100 100th Street, Urbandale, IA 50322
515/287/2144 800/557/2144 landauerpub.com

President/Publisher: Jeramy Lanigan Landauer
Editor: Doris Brunnette
Art Director: Laurel Albright
Graphic Designer: Sharon Holland
Photographers: Sue Voegtlin, Sharon Holland, and Susan Playsted

Library of Congress Control Number: 2017952648

ISBN: 978-1-935726-97-5

This book printed on acid-free paper.
Printed in United States

10-9-8-7-6-5-4-3-2-1

Landauer Books are distributed
to the Trade by
Fox Chapel Publishing
1970 Broad Street
East Petersburg, PA 17520
www.foxchapelpublishing.com
1-800-457-9112

For consumer orders:
Landauer Publishing, LLC
3100 100th Street
Urbandale, Iowa 50322
www.landauerpub.com
1-800-557-2144

Utility-Style

QUILTS FOR EVERYDAY LIVING

This book is dedicated to my family and
friends who've been my constant light
and guiding star. Thank you for your love
and patient support.

sharon holland

CONTENTS

"Regularity, order, desire for perfection
destroy art. Irregularity is the basis of all art."
—Pierre-Auguste Renoir

INTRODUCTION

Everyday use and functionality is the true meaning of *Utility-Style*. A quilt put into service, laundered, and eventually worn to threads is loved. For the patterns in this book, I challenge you to remove the expectation for perfection and embrace utility and its unexpected, fail-proof, scrappy beauty. As Pierre-Auguste Renoir once said, "Regularity, order, desire for perfection destroy art. Irregularity is the basis of all art." Likewise, Leo Tolstoy eloquently said, "If you look for perfection, you'll never be content." Embrace these words when selecting fabrics and block arrangements and you will find freedom as an artist. Unlike show quilts that are sewn to be admired on a wall or saved for special occasions like creative trophies, utility quilts are born from a humbler beginning. Once liberated of the need for flawlessness the quilter is free to experiment without pressure, make mistakes, and more importantly, use without worry.

This book welcomes you with a dozen designs inspired by timeless quilt block patterns. Create cozy quilts using surprising fabric and color combinations to put a new spin on tradition – making each quilt eternally modern. The patterns herein are fast-pieced and great for beginners. You will find the quilts range from simple-pieced to more involved patchwork blocks as well as skill-building design tips and innovative suggestions for expanding upon the samples. The projects vary in size from baby quilts to queen size quilts. If you like a design but want it smaller make fewer blocks. Likewise, if you desire a larger quilt make more blocks. The beauty of a scrap quilt is that no one will know if you've run out of fabric and had to make substitutions!

Fabric requirements in this book are written for the stated size sample. Yardage is given in total increments because some quilts incorporate material from garments, vintage, or stash fabrics that range in width. The fabrics you select therefore may vary, so a total yardage is helpful when gathering materials.

As you stitch your quilts from start to finish using this book remember to free yourself of the idealism of the perfect quilt. Instead, experiment with color, print, and block orientation, and embrace the quirkiness that comes from working with scrap and stash materials. Most of all enjoy living with your usably-modern quilts everyday!

SEWING SUPPLIES

There are a multitude of gadgets and tools on the market with the quilt maker in mind. These are the essentials recommended for successful patchwork sewing. See Quilting, page 67, for additional list of quilting supplies.

BASIC SEWING SUPPLIES

Rotary cutter, mat, and acrylic ruler – A rotary cutter and cutting mat work in conjunction with acrylic rulers. These tools are designed to cut layers of fabric quickly and accurately. The projects in this book all begin with cutting strips of fabric with a rotary cutter. A large self-healing cutting mat will protect your work surface and provide a grid ruler for cutting and squaring up fabric. Clear acrylic rulers are thicker than standard rulers and come in many shapes and sizes. Choose rulers with 1/8" increments. Selecting a 24" long ruler 6" wide or larger and a 6-1/2" or larger square ruler are good sizes to start with.

Sewing Machine – A sewing machine that sews an accurate 1/4" seam is a must for quilting. Make sure your machine is in good working order with proper thread tension for durable seam construction. Having the ability to sew with the needle in the down position is advantageous to better piecing. Attachments like a walking foot or darning foot are helpful when machine quilting on a sewing machine.

Thread – Use high quality thread for long-lasting seams and less lint deposits in your sewing machine. Choose a neutral thread color for piecing. I like to use a medium 50-weight thread for patchwork sewing and machine quilting. For piecing cotton, 100% cotton thread is best and a poly-blend or 100% polyester thread is recommended for machine quilting.

Needles – Select an all-purpose or quilting needle for your sewing machine. Change the needle often (after every big project) for best machine performance. Never sew over pins. Instead, stop with the needle in the down position, remove the pin, and continue sewing. Signs that a needle should be changed include: skipped or uneven stitches, a popping sound when the needle meets the fabric, uneven or skipped stitches.

Straight Pins – Quilting pins are long with a thin shaft and sharp point.

Scissors, Shears, and Seam Ripper – Fabric scissors and shears should be kept separate from household scissors and used only for fabric. Cutting paper and other materials can dull the blades. Shears are generally longer than scissors and meant to cut thicker fabrics. Having a small pair of sharp scissors and a pair of 8" dressmakers shears should be part of any sewing room. Because mistakes happen you'll also want to have a seam ripper available for tearing out seams.

Iron and Pressing Surface – A clean, hot iron and pressing surface is a must. Iron fabrics before cutting and during piecing.

Marking Tools – There are many fabric marking tools on the market. Water or air soluble, ceramic lead, and chalk are most common. Read and follow the manufacturer's directions for best results.

Miscellaneous – A yardstick or metal tape measure is handy for measuring fabric for backing, determining finished border sizing, and measuring binding.

A design wall is not essential but is helpful--especially when piecing a scrap quilt. You can purchase a pre-made design wall or make your own inexpensive design wall using a flannel-backed vinyl tablecloth. If making your own, use the largest rectangular or square tablecloth you can find. Or use two tablecloths side by side. Tack the tablecloth to a wall or board with the flannel side facing out. Search design wall inspiration via the web for additional ideas.

COLOR THEORY

Vintage utility quilts captivate even today's quilters with unexpected pops of color and fabric placement. Whether the design choices for these quilts were born out of necessity—using whatever surplus of materials were on hand—or from intentional artistic expression, or a bit of both, we can only speculate. Today's quilters have access to an array of fabrics like never before. It's safe to assume that today's modern utility quilts are cleverly crafted to convey the effortless thrift look of vintage scrap quilts.

COLOR

Before you can break the rules to keep your quilt looking fresh and unexpected it is helpful to understand a few basic color conventions. Understanding some basic terms when working with color will help with fabric selection for the projects in this book.

Hue – The pure spectrum name given to a color. Color scheme principles include:

Primary – Colors that cannot be produced by mixing other colors. The primary colors are red, blue, and yellow.

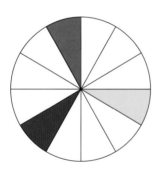

Primary

Secondary – Colors made from mixing two primary colors. The secondary colors are orange, violet, and green.

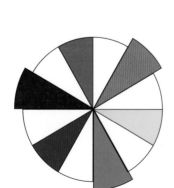

Secondary

Tertiary – Made by mixing adjacent primary and secondary hues. Called by the primary color name first, followed by the secondary hue name. Example: red-orange, red-violet, yellow-green, yellow-orange, blue-violet, blue-green.

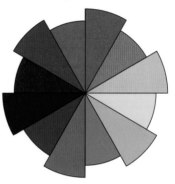

Tertiary

Complimentary – Two hues directly opposite each other on the color wheel.

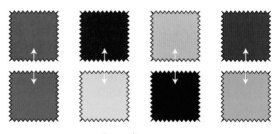

Complimentary

Triad – Three hues spaced equal distance from each other (forming an equilateral triangle on a color wheel). See more on page 13.

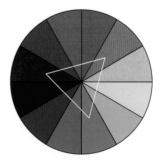

Triad

10

Split Complimentary – A hue and the colors on either side of hue's complimentary color on the color wheel.

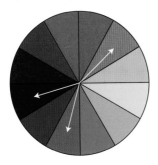

Split Complimentary

Diad – Two colors that are two colors apart on the color wheel. Example: Yellow and green, blue-violet and red-violet, etc. See more on page 13.

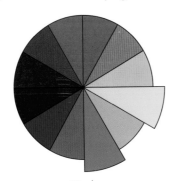

Diad

Tetrad – Two pairs of complimentary colors that form a rectangle on the color wheel. Example: Orange, yellow-green, blue, and red-violet.

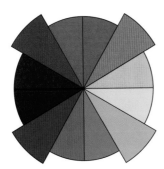

Tetrad

Analogous – Any number of hues directly next to each other on the color wheel. See more on page 13.

Analogous

Monochromatic – Color scheme limited to one hue and the multitude variations of that colors shade, tint, value, and saturation.

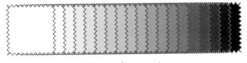

Monochromatic

Achromatic – A colorless scheme using whites, grays, and blacks.

Achromatic

VALUE

The lightness or darkness of a color. Value can create mood. For example, bright colors evoke energy and movement, whereas soft values generate a soothing effect.

SATURATION

The amount of intensity a color has describes the purity of the hue. The purer the hue the more saturated the color will be. Using fabrics of similar saturation in a quilt will make even a low-volume (light fabrics of little saturation and contrast) feel bright and balanced.

CONTRAST

The relative lightness or darkness of colors next to each other. Contrast can help define positive and negative space. Use contrast for adding to or detracting from the graphic elements in a quilt design. Contrast is highly effective for establishing hierarchy (order of importance) and composition. Like value and saturation, contrast sets a mood or tone for the quilt.

Scrap quilts invite the viewer to explore the quilt surface. Whether a quilt is made in all solids, all prints, or a combination of the two, a variety of fabrics keeps the eye moving around the quilt.

Do not be afraid of running out of a fabric in your quilt. In fact, substitutions are a welcome addition to a utility scrap quilt. Choose additional material of similar value to extend the used up fabric. Or, intentionally start with fabrics of similar values. See the *Utility-Style Tips* on each project for additional ways to add your own look to the projects in this book. Another way to substitute with interest is to pull fabrics with colors on either side of the color wheel. For example, if the focus is on a red fabric, then substitute analogous fabrics from the red-orange to orange hues and/or fabrics from the red-violet to violet hues.

CHOOSING FABRIC

MATERIAL
Understanding woven fabric will help when working with scraps or using repurposed garment fabrics in quilts anywhere a selvage edge is not apparent. See also Fabric and Quilt Care on page 45.

Selvage – Means self edge, and it is produced during weaving, finishing the edges of the fabric while on the loom. Selvages run parallel to the length of the fabric. It's important to remove the selvage edge from patchwork pieces because it shrinks at a different rate than the woven fabric.

Warp and Weft – The warp threads run parallel to the selvage edges and are the strongest fibers with the least amount of stretch. Warp fibers are called the straight-of-grain. Weft threads run perpendicular to the warp threads and are drawn through the warp threads in an over-and-under method to make woven fabric. Weft threads are also considered straight-of-grain but have a slight stretch compared to the warp threads.

Bias – Diagonal grain of fabric that is a 45° angle to the selvages. Fabric cut on a bias has considerable stretch.

SCALE
Scale is the size of a print compared to another print. Small prints can read as a solid or blender from a distance. Changing up the scale of prints within a quilt adds movement, energy, and interest. Patterned fabric brings a visual texture to your work as well as aids in color scheme selection. See more on next page.

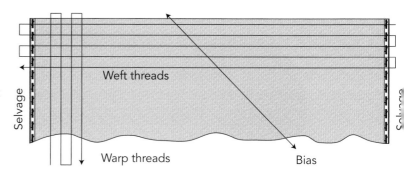

Weft threads

Selvage

Selvage

Warp threads

Bias

Analogous

Diad

Triad

ANALOGOUS
Any number of hues directly next to each other on the color wheel.

Analogous Blenders
Blenders are small prints of minimal coloring that act more like a solid than a busy print. If you squint your eyes, the print and colors merge and blend together. The example on the left shows an analogous color scheme of blue, green, and yellow which are directly next to each other on the color wheel. An analogous color scheme can contain as many colors as you wish along with the shade, tone, and tint of those colors.

DIAD
Two colors, spaced two colors apart on the color wheel.

Dot-like Prints Large to Small
A diad color scheme is different from analogous because instead of including colors from hues directly next to each other on the color wheel, a diad palette excludes the color between a pair of hues. For the example, red and violet are the colors for this palette and red-violet has been left out of this mix. Geometric prints, such as dots, make for a graphic quilt. Varying the types of dot prints in composition and ranging from large to small adds visual texture and interest to this group. The addition of a warm gray and neutral black makes this palette very modern feeling.

TRIAD
Three hues spaced equal distance from each other on the color wheel.

Triad Large to Small Mixed Prints
Finding new and unusual color stories for quilts is easy using color theory. Yellow-orange, blue-green, and red-violet was the starting point for picking this group of 12 prints. Selecting different scaled prints from large to small as well as mixing florals and geometric blender prints all add interest and texture to the fabric pull.

The introduction to this book talks about letting go of the conventions of perfection when creating utility quilts. This doesn't mean abandoning accurate sewing practices. Exact cutting and piecing are essential for successful patchwork and will make your quilt making experience an enjoyable one.

Written with the beginner in mind, this book contains all the information needed to cut, sew, and finish a dozen different utility quilts. The methods and techniques given to complete the projects are my methods of sewing patchwork. Although there are other ways to reach the same end result, I've found these techniques lend themselves nicely to achieving the random, scrappy look desired when working with a multitude of fabrics.

PATCHWORK BASICS

CUTTING STRIPS

All the projects in this book are assembled from first cutting strips on the cross grain from selvage to selvage. The strips are then sub-cut into smaller pieces or sewn together to make binding, borders, or sashing. Using a rotary cutter, rotary cutting mat, and acrylic ruler are essential for making straight and accurate pieces.

1. Press fabric. Fold the fabric in half with selvage edges matched. Place the folded fabric on the cutting mat with the fold edge nearest to you and ample mat area extending beyond the fabric. Note: If working on a small mat, you may need to fold the fabric twice so the first folded edge is even with the selvage edges and the second double-fold is nearest to you.

2. Place a square ruler on top of the fabric with the edge of the ruler aligned with the fold closest to you and near the left edge of the fabric raw edges (on the right edge if left-handed). Position the long side of a 24" ruler against the left edge of the square ruler overlapping the raw edge by at least 1/2".

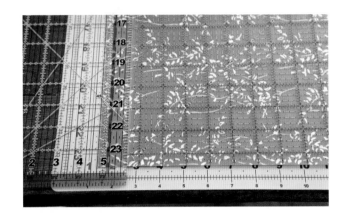

3. Carefully slide the square ruler out of the way while keeping your left hand firmly on the long ruler. Note: The raw edge of the fabric should be completely under the long ruler.

4. Hold the rotary cutter next to the right edge of the long ruler and roll the cutter away from you using a firm, downward pressure while cutting through the layers of fabric. Walk your fingers up the ruler as needed to keep the ruler from slipping.

5. Remove the trimmed starting edge without disturbing the straightened edge of fabric and you're ready to begin cutting strips.

6. Cut width of strips according to pattern by aligning the vertical markings on the long ruler with the straightened fabric edge, using the horizontal markings for the desired width. Cut in the same manner as in Step 4. Note: To cut strips wider than your ruler you will need to use two rulers to achieve the desired strip width. If you are left-handed the steps for rotary cutting are the same; except you cut from the right side of the fabric instead of the left. Watch a demonstration of these techniques at landauerpub.com/videos/fabricprep.html.

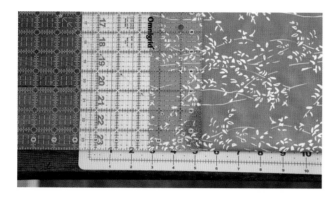

SUB-CUTTING STRIPS

Cutting quilt block pieces from strips is a time-saver and makes the piecing process easy because you're working with accurate pieces. Once you're familiar with the process you can cut up to 4 layers of fabric at a time, if desired.

Place a folded strip on the cutting mat in front of you horizontally with folded edge on your right (on the left if left-handed). Use a ruler to square-off the ends of the strip, removing the selvage edges.

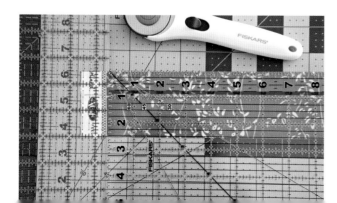

In the same manner as in Cutting the Strips, align the straighten edge of the strip with the ruler marking that corresponds to the length of piece indicated on the pattern. Cut the number of pieces needed from the fabric strip(s), opening the folded end, if necessary, to cut a single layer of fabric.

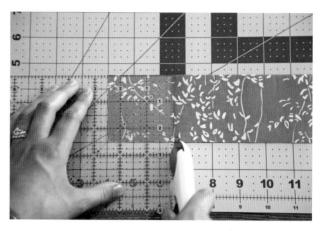

WORKING WITH DIRECTIONAL PRINTS

When direction matters, think about fabric placement and cutting before you begin.

Strips are cut on the straight-of-grain from selvage to selvage. If your print is directional and it matters for your quilt design to keep it directional, you will want to inverse the strip cutting measurements in some cases. Obviously, a square piece can be rotated during piecing to accommodate directional prints but a rectangle may not be oriented correctly for your needs. If that is the case, adapt the following example when cutting your pieces:

-If the cutting instructions call for a (1) 3" x 42" strip to then be cut into (6) 3" x 6" rectangles you would instead cut (1) 6" x 42" strip and then cut into (6) 6" x 3" (directional) rectangles.

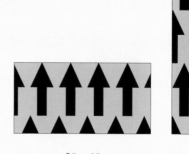

3" x 6"   6" x 3"

SEAM ALLOWANCE

The cutting instructions in this book include a 1/4" seam allowance on all sides. *Finished block* or *finished size* refers to a block once it's sewn together. This measurement no longer includes the seam allowances. A finished quilt can vary in size from the pattern dimensions due to variations in sewing, quilting, and shrinkage after laundering. I've rounded the quilt project finished sizes down to the nearest whole number but all the projects include an additional 1/2" to their final dimensions because the outside edge of each quilt, even though finished with binding, still remains part of the overall finished dimensions.

Checking the accuracy of your 1/4" seam allowance before you start sewing is an important first step in piecing patchwork. If your seam allowance is too wide or too narrow these small amounts can add up to significant differences when piecing the blocks and assembling a quilt. Stitching with a 1/4" presser foot does not guarantee an accurate seam allowance and a check should be done to understand what adjustments, if any, are needed before beginning your patchwork project.

An easy way to see if your sewing machine is hitting the 1/4" mark is to place a sheet of quarter-inch rule graph paper under the needle on your machine and lower the needle to where two perpendicular lines intersect. If the right edge of the presser foot aligns with the closest quarter-inch mark no further action is needed. Proceed to Piecing on next page.

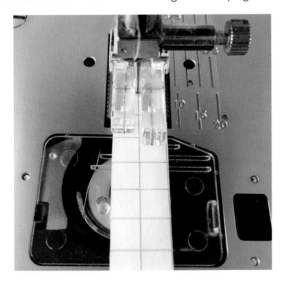

If the right edge of the presser foot extends beyond the nearest quarter-inch mark and your machine has the ability to move the needle side to side, adjust the needle position to the left until the right side of the presser foot aligns at the quarter-inch mark. Make note of this adjustment and reset your needle position each time you need a 1/4" seam allowance for sewing. If the initial test shows the presser foot to the left of the mark move the needle position to the right to adjust placement.

If you are unable to re-position your sewing machine needle, place a piece of tape on your sewing machine throat plate as a guide to keep the edge of your patchwork straight and aligned for accurate 1/4" seam allowances.

Carefully cut an 1/2" x 6" piece of quarter-inch graph paper.

Drop needle down 1-1/2" in from one short end of the graph paper strip and centered on intersected perpendicular lines.

Adjust the paper guide so the edge is parallel to the lines on the throat plate. Position tape along the right (the long side) of the guide, abutting the edges. Raise the presser foot and needle to remove the paper guide. Align fabric to the left edge of the tape guide for an accurate 1/4" seam allowance.

SEAM ALLOWANCE TEST

Using a rotary cutter, rotary mat, and acrylic ruler, follow the steps in Cutting Strips on page 14 and the steps on Sub-Cutting Strips page 15 for the following seam allowance test then accurately cut (2) 4-1/2" squares and (1) 4-1/2" x 8-1/2" rectangle.

Sew the (2) 4-1/2" squares right sides together (see Piecing and Pinning on page 17). Set the seam by pressing the stitching line then opening the unit and pressing seams toward one side, see Pressing on page 17. The section should measure 4-1/2" x 8-1/2". If too large, then your seam allowance is too narrow. If the unit is too small then the seam allowance is too wide. Adjust your needle position or guides accordingly.

After your seam allowance has been adjusted and the section measures 4-1/2" x 8-1/2" exactly, sew the 4-1/2" x 8-1/2" rectangle to the squares section. Set the seam and press seams toward the rectangle. Results should be a perfect 8-1/2" square.

PIECING

The quilt projects in this book are designed for the beginner. The pieces are all simple, four-sided shapes for easy piecing. All pieces are sewn right sides together using a 1/4" seam allowance. Pinning and matching edges before sewing will improve accuracy, making for sharp points and neat corners. Follow the step-by-step instructions for sewing units, sections, and blocks.

PINNING

The general rule is to press the seams in one direction toward the darkest fabric. However, for some of the projects in this book I suggest you press the seams open for easier assembly. Nesting seams before sewing means the seam allowances of each unit are going in the opposite direction. If working with seam allowances that have been pressed open make sure all edges match and stitching lines meet.

Pinning helps to keep pieces and units from shifting when sewing. Pin nested seam allowances on a diagonal from right to left as shown, locking the seams in place. Do not sew over pins. Instead, stitch up to the diagonally placed pin, catching the leading seam allowance. With the needle in the down position, stop and remove the pin before proceeding.

PRESSING

When piecing you'll want to press not iron. Pressing is the motion of picking the iron up and putting it down rather than sliding it across the surface. When pressing a unit or a block press the seam from the back first to set the seam then press the piece open. Press as you piece so the block stays true to size.

When pressing, direction is important. Place the fabric the seam allowance is to be pressed toward face up when pressing and opening. This trick will save time and result in the seams being pressed in the direction of the face-up fabric.

I do not recommend using a steam iron, unless you have a professional grade steam iron. Moisture can distort the shape of pieces. Use the correct setting for the type of material and keep the iron clean. If working with hard to handle laundered fabrics or stretchy bias edge shapes, using a spray starch product while pressing will stabilize the material and give it body for easier handling.

Cabin

This simple Log Cabin design is reminiscent of the colorful bands found on Hudson Bay blankets. The bright red-orange center ring welcomes you like an open doorway to a comfortable home.

UTILITY STYLE TIP

Add even more interest to this graphic quilt design by using fabrics of similar hues in the concentric rings. Try inversing the light and dark rings for a completely different look.

Finished Size: 54" square

MATERIAL

1-5/8 yards off-white print

5/8 yard green print

1/2 yard gold print

1/3 yard yellow solid

1 fat quarter red-orange print

1/2 yard charcoal solid
for binding

3-1/2 yards backing

62" square batting

Read through all instructions before beginning. Sew pieces right sides together and use a 1/4"seam allowance throughout unless otherwise stated.

NOTE

If working with strips of fabrics with similar hues for the concentric rows, join the strips into one long strip by sewing short ends right sides together using a 1/4" seam allowance. Press seams open to reduce bulk. From the cutting instructions, cut one long strip then one adjacent shorter strip in the square. Repeat in that order to achieve a continuous material look when piecing. If using the same material for the various squares, sew strips into one long strip for each color, press then follow the cutting instructions in the cut order as written.

CUTTING

From off-white print, cut:
(1) 6-1/2" square

(13) 3-1/2" x 42" strip (or 546" total length). Join strips end to end to make one long strip. Press seams open. From strip, cut:
    (2) 3-1/2" x 54-1/2" strips,
    (2) 3-1/2" x 48-1/2" strips,
    (2) 3-1/2" x 42-1/2" strips,
    (2) 3-1/2" x 36-1/2" strips,
    (2) 3-1/2" x 30-1/2" strips,
    (2) 3-1/2" x 24-1/2" strips,
    (2) 3-1/2" x 18-1/2" strips,
    (2) 3-1/2" x 12-1/2" strips.

From green print, cut:
(5) 3-1/2" x 42" strips (or 210" total length). Join strips end to end to make one long strip. Press seams open. From strip, cut:
    (2) 3-1/2" x 48-1/2" strips,
    (2) 3-1/2" x 42-1/2" strips.

From gold print, cut:
(4) 3-1/2" x 42" strips (or 168" total length).
    From strips, cut:
    (2) 3-1/2" x 36-1/2" strips,
    (2) 3-1/2" x 30-1/2" strips.

From yellow solid, cut:
(3) 3-1/2" x 42" strips (or 126" total length).
    From strips, cut:
    (2) 3-1/2" x 24-1/2" strips,
    (2) 3-1/2" x 18-1/2" strips.

From red-orange print, cut:
(3) 3-1/2" x 21" strips (or 63" total length).
    From strips, cut:
    (2) 3-1/2" x 12-1/2" strips,
    (2) 3-1/2" x 6-1/2" strips.

From charcoal solid, cut:
(6) 2-1/4" x 42" strips (or 252" total length) for binding.

QUILT ASSEMBLY

1. Sew (2) 3-1/2" x 6-1/2" red-orange strips to opposite sides of the 6-1/2" off-white square. Sew (2) 3-1/2" x 12-1/2" red-orange strips to the remaining sides of center square.

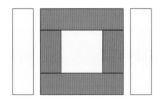

2. Sew (2) 3-1/2" x 12-1/2" off-white strips to the opposite sides of the center unit. Sew (2) 3-1/2" x 18-1/2" off-white strips to the remaining sides.

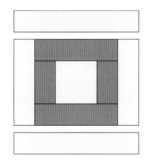

3. Referring to the Quilt Assembly Diagram on page 21, continue to add rows in the same manner, alternating between colored strips and background strips.

FINISHING

1. Cut backing fabric into two 1-3/4 yard pieces. Cut selvages off and join together, using a 1/2" seam allowance. Press seam and trim to 62" square. Layer the backing, batting and quilt top. Baste all layers together.

2. Refer to Quilting and Finishing on page 67 for finishing the quilt. Use the (6) 2-1/4"-wide charcoal solid strips for binding.

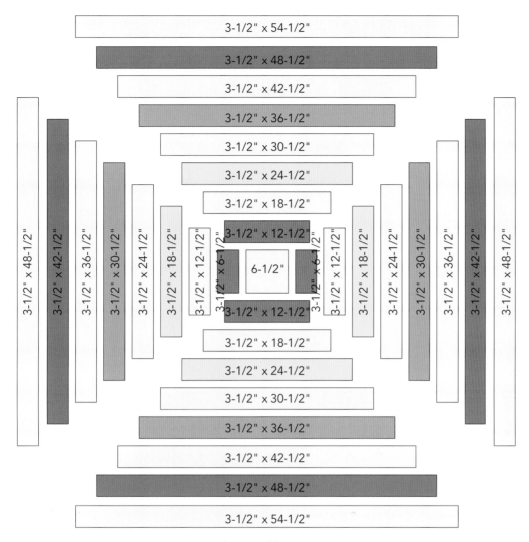

Quilt Assembly Diagram

Elbow Quilting Diagram

REPEAT QUILT PATTERNS

Repeating quilt patterns provide an additional overall texture to the quilt. This type of quilt design needs to be drawn onto the quilt top before basting. Use the marking tool as instructed. Marking out a top is labor intensive but the time spent will be made up when quilting directly onto the markings.

Refer to Elbow Pattern on page 71 for stitching the utility quilt design used on the *Cabin* quilt.

Tracery

This is a great project for playing with value, saturation, and contrast. Light prints visually float the darker and more saturated petal-like block centers on the low-volume background.

UTILITY STYLE TIP

Depending upon the placement of light and dark, this block has the potential for a lot of versatility. The center of the design can be arranged like the sample or the dark pieced area can be extended to replace some of the light strips to fool the eye into thinking different-sized blocks were used. Mixing up the size of the centers will create even more movement in this quilt.

Finished Size: 63" square

Finished Block: 21" square

MATERIAL

3/8 yard **each** of 12 light prints/solids (or 4-1/2 yards total) includes binding

1/4 yard **each** of 12 dark prints/solids

4 yards backing

71" square batting

Read through all instructions before beginning. Sew pieces right sides together and use a 1/4" seam allowance throughout unless otherwise stated.

CUTTING

From each of the 12 light prints/solids, cut:
(3) 3-1/2" 42" strips. From strips cut a total of:
(18) assorted 3-1/2" x 21-1/2" strips,
(18) assorted 3-1/2" x 15-1/2" strips,
(18) assorted 3-1/2" x 9-1/2" strips,
(36) assorted 3-1/2" x 8" strips.

(7) 2-1/4" -wide assorted strips (or 264" total length) for binding

From each of 5 dark prints/solid, cut:
(1) 3-1/2" x 42" strip. From strip cut:
    (9) 3-1/2" squares,
    (4) 2" x 3-1/2" rectangles.

(2) 2" x 42" strip. From strip cut:
    (3) 2" x 9-1/2" strips,
    (5) 2" x 6-1/2" strips.

From each of the remaining 7 dark prints/solids, cut:
(2) 2" x 42" strips. From strips cut:
    (2) 2" x 9-1/2" strips,
    (7) 2" x 6-1/2" strips.

BLOCK ASSEMBLY

1. Sew 2 assorted 2" x 3-1/2" dark print/solid rectangles to opposite sides of a dark 3-1/2" square. Press toward rectangles. Add 2 assorted 2" x 6-1/2" dark print/solid strips to the remaining sides of the center square. Press seam allowance toward the piece just added in each following step.

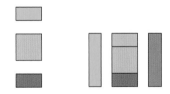

2. Stitch 2 assorted 2" x 6-1/2" dark print/solid strips to opposite sides of center unit. Press. Sew 2 assorted 2" x 9-1/2" dark print/solid strips to the remaining sides of the unit. Press.

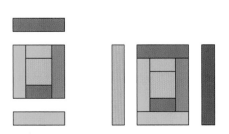

3. Draw a diagonal line on the wrong side of a 3-1/2" dark print/solid square. Place the square right sides together on one corner of the center unit, aligning raw edges. Stitch on the drawn line, trim 1/4" beyond line. Press the corner out. Repeat for remaining corners.

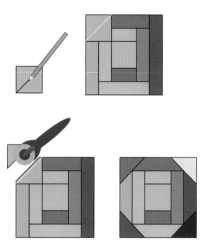

4. Sew (2) 3-1/2" x 9-1/2" light print/solid strips to opposite sides of the center section. Sew 2 assorted 3-1/2" x 8" strips together end-to-end. Stitch the pieced strip to one of the remaining sides of the center section. Repeat for remaining side of the center section.

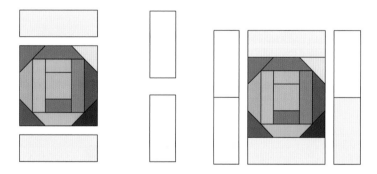

5. Stitch 2 assorted 3-1/2" x 15-1/2" light print/solid strips to opposite sides of the center section. Stitch (2) 3-1/2" x 21-1/2" assorted light print/solid strips to the remaining sides to complete block. Make 9 blocks.

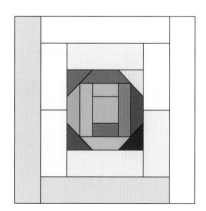

QUILT ASSEMBLY
1. Referring to Quilt Assembly Diagram on page 25, arrange blocks in 3 rows of 3 blocks each. Note how the orientation of the blocks alternate.

2. Join the blocks into rows. Join rows together to complete quilt top.

FINISHING
1. Cut backing fabric into two 2 yard pieces. Cut selvages off and join together using a 1/2" seam allowance. Press seam and trim to 71" square. Layer the backing, batting and quilt top. Baste all layers together.

2. Refer to Quilting and Finishing on page 67 for finishing the quilt. See Fan pattern on page 71 to quilt as the sample. Use the 2-1/4"-wide assorted light prints/solid strips (or 264" total) for binding.

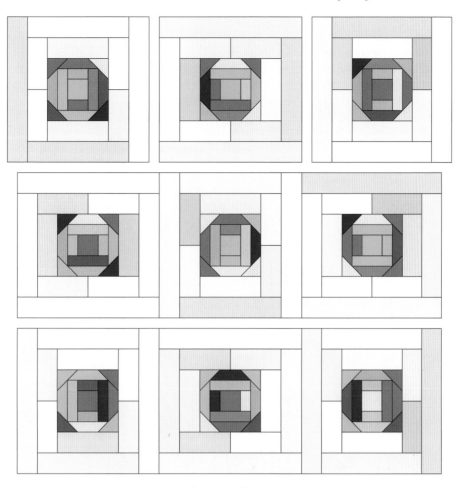

Quilt Assembly Diagram

Hawthorn

Designs with simple, graphic blocks will never go out of style. The traditional Anvil block complements just about any décor. Splitting the side blocks gives the quilt an intentional naïve quality that exemplifies utility style.

UTILITY STYLE TIP
This quilt uses only six different fabrics but gives the impression of being more complex. It is a great starter project for anyone overwhelmed by the selection of many fabrics. Graphic pops of contrasting lights and darks scattered between mid-value fabrics simplifies the selection process.

Finished Size: 81" x 84"

Finished Block: 24" square

MATERIAL
3 yards orange print

1-1/8 yards off-white solid

7/8 yard light tan print

2/3 yard navy print

2/3 yard yellow print

1-1/4 yards large bloom print

5/8 yard rust solid for binding

7-1/2 yards backing

89" x 92" batting

Read through all instructions before beginning. Sew pieces right sides together and use a 1/4" seam allowance throughout unless otherwise stated.

Changing the fabric placement and contrast, as well as the number of prints/solids in a block, adds to the scrappy utility look of this quilt. The following piecing instructions are for making the quilt as shown. Feel free to experiment with new combinations.

CUTTING
From orange print, cut:
(1) 12-1/2" x 42" strip. From strip cut:
    (2) 12-1/2" squares,
    (1) 6-1/2" x 12-1/2" rectangle.

(4) 6-7/8" x 42" strips. From strips cut:
    (20) 6-7/8" squares.

(2) 6-1/2" x 42" strips. From strips cut:
    (10) 6-1/2" squares.

(13) 3-1/2" x 42" strips. From 3 strips cut:
    (8) 3-1/2" x 12-1/2" strips. Sew remaining
    3-1/2" strips together end-to-end to make one
    long strip. Press seams open then cut:
    (17) 3-1/2" x 24-1/2" strips for sashing.

From off-white solid, cut:
(3) 6-7/8" x 42" strips. From strips cut:
    (13) 6-7/8" squares.

(2) 6-1/2" x 42" strips. From strips cut:
    (1) 6-1/2" x 12-1/2" rectangle,
    (9) 6-1/2" squares.

From light tan print, cut:
(1) 12-1/2" x 42" strip. From strip cut:
    (3) 12-1/2" squares.

(2) 6-7/8" x 42" strips. From strips cut:
    (9) 6-7/8" squares,
    (1) 6-1/2" x 12-1/2" rectangle,
    (1) 6-1/2" square.

From navy print, cut:
(2) 6-7/8" x 42" strips. From strips cut:
    (12) 6-7/8" squares.

(1) 6-1/2" x 42" strip. From strip cut:
    (1) 6-1/2" x 12-1/2" rectangle,
    (4) 6-1/2" squares.

From yellow print, cut:
(2) 6-7/8" x 42" strips. From strips cut:
    (10) 6-7/8" squares.

(1) 6-1/2" x 42" strip. From strip cut:
    (1) 6-1/2" x 12-1/2" rectangle,
    (4) 6-1/2" squares.

From large bloom print, cut:
(1) 12-1/2" square.

(2) 6-7/8" x 42" strips. From strips cut:
    (8) 6-7/8" squares.

(2) 6-1/2" x 42" strips. From strips cut:
    (1) 6-1/2" x 12-1/2" rectangle,
    (8) 6-1/2" squares.

From the leftover fabric, select 4 prints, cut:
(12) 3-1/2" squares (total) for cornerstones.

From rust solid, cut:
(9) 2-1/4" x 42" strips (or 342" total length)
for binding.

BLOCK ASSEMBLY

1. Pair the 6-7/8" squares as shown to make a total of 36 pairs.

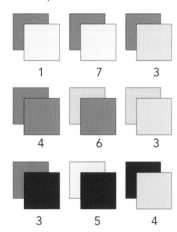

2. Draw a diagonal line on the wrong side of the lighter fabric in each pair. With each marked square and its 6-7/8" paired square right sides together, sew a 1/4" seam on each side of the drawn line. Cut apart on the line to make (2) 6-1/2" half-square triangles. Open and press seams toward the dark print. Trim dog ears. Make a total of 72 half-square triangles.

3. Lay out (1) 12-1/2" square, 8 half-square triangles, and (4) 6-1/2" squares as shown. Noting placement and orientation, sew pieces into 3 rows. Join the rows to complete a block. Make a total of 6 full blocks.

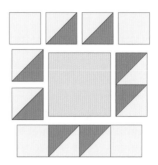

4. For the half block blocks, lay out (1) 6-1/2" x 12-1/2" rectangle, (4) half-square triangles, and (2) 6-1/2" squares as shown. Noting placement and orientation, sew pieces into 3 rows. Join the rows to complete a half-block. Make a total of 6 half-blocks.

QUILT ASSEMBLY

1. Referring to the Quilt Assembly Diagram, page 29, sew (3) 3-1/2" squares alternately between (2) 3-1/2" x 12-1/2" orange print strips and (2) 3-1/2" x 24-1/2" orange print strips. Make a total of 4 sashing rows.

2. Stitch (3) 3-1/2" x 24-1/2" orange print strips alternately between 2 half blocks and 2 full blocks. Make a total of 3 block rows.

3. Stitch the sashing and block rows together.

FINISHING

1. Cut backing fabric into three 2-1/2 yard pieces. Cut selvages off and join together lengthwise using a 1/2" seam allowance. Press seam open and trim to 89" x 92". Layer the backing, batting and quilt top. Baste all layers together.

2. Refer to Quilting and Finishing on page 67 for finishing the quilt. Use Orange Peel quilting pattern, page 29. Use the (9) 2-1/4"-wide rust solid strips (or 342" total length) for binding.

Quilt Assembly Diagram

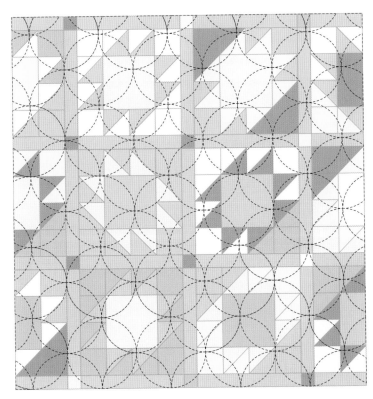

Orange Peel Quilting Diagram

REPEAT QUILT PATTERNS

Repeating quilt patterns provide an additional overall texture to the quilt. This type of quilt design needs to be drawn onto the quilt top before basting. Use the marking tool as instructed. Marking out a top is labor intensive but the time spent will be made up when quilting directly onto the markings.

Refer to Quilting on page 72 for stitching the Orange Peel utility quilt design used on the *Hawthorn* quilt.

Viewpoint

Inspired by a homespun linen dish towel, half-square triangle edges frame the striped pieced center of this table runner. The monochromatic palette unifies the fabrics and reads more as one fabric from afar.

UTILITY STYLE TIP

Depending upon your style, this runner can quietly complement a room or demand attention. Just imagine how different it would look with a large-scale print. Keep the palette within the same hue as shown in the monochromatic sample or use two or three hue complements from the color wheel to enliven the palette.

Finished Size: 16" x 70"

MATERIAL

1 yard gold solid

3/8 yard white solid

1/2 yard light stripe
(includes binding)

1/4 yard **each** of 4 assorted
gold prints (or 1 yard total)

1-1/3 yards backing

24" x 78" batting

Read through all instructions before beginning. Sew pieces right sides together and use a 1/4" seam allowance throughout unless otherwise stated.

CUTTING

From gold solid, cut:
(4) 5" x 42" strips. From strips cut:
    (12) 5" x 11-1/2" strips.

(2) 2-7/8" x 42" strips. From strips cut:
    (20) 2-7/8" squares.

(3) 1-1/2" x 42" strips. From strips cut:
    (9) 1-1/2" x 11-1/2" strips.

From white solid, cut:
(3) 2-7/8" x 42" strips. From strips cut:
    (40) 2-7/8" squares.

(2) 2-1/2" squares.

From light stripe, cut:
(1) 2-7/8" x 42" strip. From strip cut:
    (5) 2-7/8" squares.

(5) 2-1/4" x 42" strips for binding.

(1) 1-1/2" x 42" strip. From strip cut a total of:
    (2) 1-1/2" x 11-1/2" strips.

From assorted gold prints, cut a total of:
(15) 3-7/8" squares

(7) 1-1/2" x 11-1/2" strips.

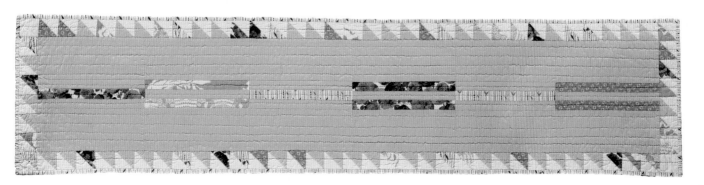

RUNNER ASSEMBLY

1. Draw a diagonal line on the wrong side of each 2-7/8" white solid square. Place a marked square, right sides together, on a 2-7/8" gold solid, striped, or assorted gold print square. Sew a 1/4" seam on each side of the drawn line. Cut apart on the line to make (2) 2-1/2" half-square triangles. Open and press seams toward the gold fabric. Trim dog ears. Make a total of (80) square half-square triangles.

2. Sew a 1-1/2" x 11-1/2" gold solid strip between (2) 1-1/2" x 11-1/2" matching gold print strips as shown. Sew a 5" x 11-1/2" gold solid strip to each long side of the center strip unit to make an A block. Make a total of 3 A blocks.

3. Sew a 1-1/2" x 11-1/2" assorted gold print or stripe strip between (2) 1-1/2" x 11-1/2" gold solid strips as shown. Sew a 5" x 11-1/2" gold solid strip to each long side of this center strip unit to make a B block. Make a total of 3 B blocks.

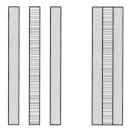

 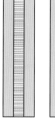  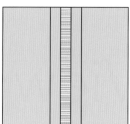

4. Referring to the Runner Assembly Diagram on page 33, join the A and B blocks into a row, alternating placement of the blocks.

5. Noting orientation, sew 33 half-square triangles together into one long side border as shown. Make a total of 2 long side borders. Sew a border to each long side of the runner center.

6. Sew 7 half-square triangles and (1) 2-1/2" white solid square together as shown. Make a total of 2 short borders. Stitch a short border to each end of the runner.

FINISHING

1. Cut backing into two 24" x 42" pieces. Cut selvages off and join pieces at the narrow end, using a 1/2" seam allowance. Press seam open. Layer the backing, batting and quilt top. Baste all layers together.

2. Refer to Quilting and Finishing on page 67 for finishing the quilt. To hand quilt, use quilting thread for thin traditional looking stitches or use perle cotton thread for a thick, bold finish. Use the 2-1/4" -wide striped strips (or 184" total length) for binding.

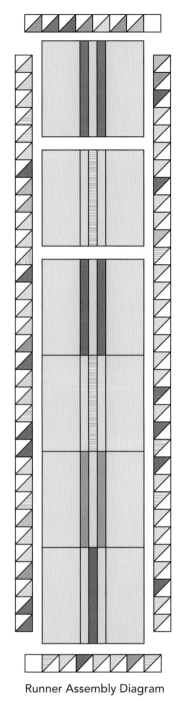

Runner Assembly Diagram

HAND QUILTING

Hand quilting is a slow process but the irregular beauty of the stitches gives a quilt a traditional look and wonderful drape.

Utilizing a hand-held hoop for small projects and a large stand-up hoop or frame for bed-size quilts will make handling and stitching easier. Place the basted quilt sandwich in a hoop or frame and tighten. Thread a Between needle with an 18'' length of thread. Knot the end of the thread and insert the needle into the quilt top and batting only a few inches away from where you intend to start quilting. Tug on the thread until the knot goes through the quilt top and is embedded in the batting. Tip: Place your index finger next to the knot. Holding the quilt top fabric taught while tugging will help support the fabric and reduce "bruising" when burying the knot.

Position the quilt so you can stitch toward yourself or away from your dominant hand. Make a running stitch by holding the needle between your thumb and index finger. Wearing a thimble on your middle finger will help push the needle through the quilt layers. Use your free hand to guide the needle from below and rock the tip of the needle to the surface of the quilt, loading the first stitch onto the needle.

Use your thumb of your needle hand to push the needle back through the layers and rock the tip of the needle back up through the layers to the surface to load a second stitch on the needle. Once 2-4 running stitches have been loaded onto the needle, gently pull the thread through and begin again. Don't pull the thread too tight; the stitches should indent the quilt layers and lie relaxed on the surface. Try to keep the stitches as evenly spaced as possible for a uniform look. As you stitch use your free hand to continually check the backside of the hoop, ensuring the sandwich remains smooth and free of puckers. Reposition the hoop or frame as needed to comfortably quilt within the stretched area.

End your stitching by wrapping the thread around the needle 2-3 times and close to the quilt top. Hold the tail of the thread with a slight tension and insert the needle into the ending stitch, going through the quilt top and batting only. Bring the needle back up to the quilt top surface approximately 1/2'' away from the stitching. Bury the knot in the same manner as in starting a stitch. Clip the thread close to the quilt surface. Tip: If using a contrasting quilt thread, avoid burying entry or ending knots in light colored fabrics for better concealment.

Pixel

Beginner-friendly Four Patch sections are ideal for using up scraps. Deliberate disregard for light and dark placement in orientation amplifies the interest in this throw-size quilt.

UTILITY STYLE TIP

The more, the merrier is the theme to this quilt. Even though the block construction is simple, this project is all about color placement. Bright, pure hues dominate less saturated colors, making some areas of the quilt visually recede and other areas advance.

Finished Size: 54" square

Finished Block 10" square

MATERIAL

1/2 yard tan solid for border

1 yard light gray solid

2/3 yard cream solid

1/4 yard orange solid

Fat eighths (or scraps) of 8 assorted light/medium solids/prints (1/2 yard total)

Fat eighths (or scraps) of 8 assorted medium/dark solids/prints (1/2 yard total)

1/2 yard for binding

3-1/2 yards backing

62" square batting

Read through all instructions before beginning. Sew pieces right sides together and use a 1/4" seam allowance throughout unless otherwise stated.

CUTTING

From tan solid, cut:
(6) 2-1/2" x 42" strips for borders.

From light gray solid, cut:
(2) 10-1/2" x 42" strips. From strips cut:
  (8) 10-1/2" squares.

(4) 2-1/2" x 42" strips. From strips cut:
  (32) 2-1/2" x 4-1/2" rectangles.

From cream solid, cut:
(2) 10-1/2" x 42" strips. From strips cut:
  (5) 10-1/2" squares.

From orange solid, cut:
(2) 2-1/2" x 42" strips. From strips cut:
  (16) 2-1/2" x 4-1/2" rectangles.

From the assorted solids/prints and leftover fabric from cutting above, cut a total of:
(102) pairs of 2-1/2" squares (or 204 total squares).

From the binding, cut:
(6) assorted 2-1/4" x 42" strips (or 228" total length) for binding.

BLOCK ASSEMBLY

1. Pair two pair of 2-1/2" squares as shown. Stitch squares together into 2 rows of 2 squares each, alternating fabric placement. Join rows to make 1 four-patch unit. Make 48 four-patch units.

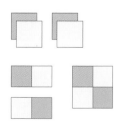

2. As shown on page 36, lay out 4 four-patch units, 4 matching 2-1/2" x 4-1/2" rectangles and one 2-1/2" square into 3 rows of 3 units/pieces each as shown. Join into rows to make 1 block. Make a total of 12 blocks.

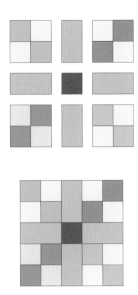

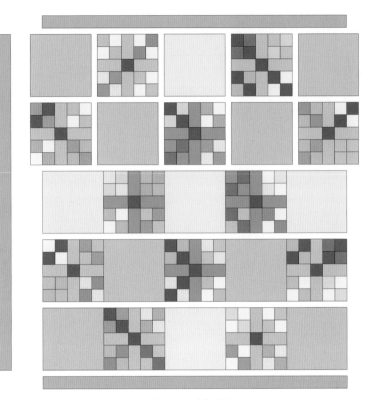

Quilt Assembly Diagram

QUILT ASSEMBLY

1. Referring to the Quilt Assembly Diagram, and noting block/square placement, lay out (13) 10-1/2" solid squares and (12) 10-1/2" four-patch blocks. Join the blocks into 5 rows of 5 blocks each. Join rows to complete the center of the quilt top.

2. Sew the (6) 2-1/2" x 42" tan solid strips together end-to-end to make one long strip. Measure opposite sides of the quilt. Average those numbers and cut 2 borders. Stitch to opposite sides of the quilt. Measure the remaining sides including the border. Average those numbers and cut a top and a bottom border to this size. Add to top and bottom of the quilt.

FINISHING

1. Cut backing fabric into two 1-3/4 yard pieces. Cut selvages off and join together using a 1/2" seam allowance. Press seam and trim to 63" square. Layer the backing, batting and quilt top. Baste all layers together.

2. Refer to Quilting and Finishing on page 67 for finishing the quilt. See Parallel Straight Line Quilting, page 70, to quilt as shown in sample. Use the (6) assorted 2-1/4"-wide strips (or 228" total length) for binding.

TYING A QUILT

Tying a quilt is an alternative to quilting. It can be used in addition to quilting to add embellishment and further stabilize the layers.

Work on a pinned, thread stitched, or spray basted quilt sandwich (See Pinning or Thread Basting page 68), tying the quilt approximately every 4" to keep all three layers secure.

Use non-divisible wool tapestry yarn or perle cotton thread and a large-eye embroidery needle. Thread the embroidery needle with an 18" long strand.

Starting at the center of the quilt, take a single stitch approximately 1/4" long through all the quilt layers beginning and ending on the top of the quilt.

Leave a 2" long thread tail on each end. Tie a square knot with the thread ends. Pull the knot tight to secure but not so tight as to pucker the quilt top. Continue across the entire quilt surface in the same manner.

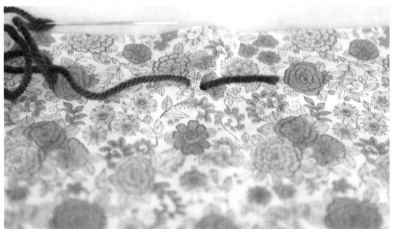

Night & Day

Night and Day was designed as a faux Log Cabin block. When the blocks are arranged as in the sample quilt, a Log Cabin arrangement traditionally called Sunshine and Shadow is created. This quilt is an excellent exercise in using contrast and value in a quilt.

UTILITY STYLE TIP

Separate your fabric selections into piles of light, medium, and dark value. Take a photograph of your selections and then view them in gray scale to see if there is enough contrast. Arrange your blocks as shown in the sample or play around with block orientation and placement for a unique design.

Finished Size: 87" square

Finished Block: 12-1/2" square

MATERIAL

1/2 yard raspberry solid for block centers

2/3 yard **each** 8 assorted light prints (5-1/3 yards total)

1/2 yard **each** 8 assorted medium/dark prints (4 yards total)

2/3 yard raspberry batik for binding

9 yards backing

95" square batting

Read through all instructions before beginning. Sew pieces right sides together and use a 1/4" seam allowance throughout unless otherwise stated.

The wavy parallel line utility quilting was quilted by Mandy Leins of Mandaleiquilts.

CUTTING

Note: If using 8 assorted light prints and 8 assorted medium/dark prints, your quilt will have more fabric variety though you'll have extra fabric. The medium prints can replace light prints for added interest, but note the light print areas require 2 more rectangles than dark areas.

From raspberry solid, cut:
(4) 3" x 42" strips. From strips cut:
    (49) 3" squares.

From each light print, cut:
(1) 5-1/2" x 42" strip. From strip cut:
    (7) 5-1/2" squares.

(5) 3" x 42" strips. From strips cut:
    (28) 3" x 5-1/2" rectangles,
    (14) 3" squares.

From each medium/dark print, cut:
(1) 5-1/2" x 42" strip. From strip cut:
    (7) 5-1/2" squares.

(3) 3" x 42" strips. From strips cut:
    (14) 3" x 5-1/2" rectangles,
    (14) 3" squares.

From raspberry batik, cut:
(9) 2-1/4" x 42" strips (or 364" total length) for binding.

BLOCK ASSEMBLY

1. Sew a 3" medium/dark print square to a 3" light print square. Press seams open. Stitch a 3" x 5-1/2" matching light print rectangle to one side. Press seams open in each following step. Make 2 identical units.

2. Sew a 3" raspberry solid square between a 3" x 5-1/2" matching light print rectangle and a 3" x 5-1/2" matching medium/dark print rectangle as

shown to make the center block row. Tip: Play with light and dark valued fabrics.

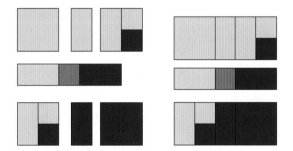

3. Stitch (1) 3" x 5-1/2" matching light print rectangle between (1) 5-1/2" matching light print square and one pieced unit. Press seams open. In the same manner, stitch (1) 3" x 5-1/2" matching medium/ dark print rectangle between (1) 5-1/2" matching medium/dark print square and one pieced unit. Join the 3 sections to make a block. Press seams open. Make a total of 49 blocks.

QUILT ASSEMBLY

1. Referring to Quilt Assembly Diagram, page 41, and noting placement and orientation, arrange blocks in 7 rows of 7 blocks.

2. Join the blocks into rows. Join rows together to complete quilt top.

FINISHING

1. Cut backing fabric into three 3 yard pieces. Cut selvages off and join together lengthwise using a 1/2" seam allowance. Press seam open and trim to 95" square. Layer the backing, batting and quilt top. Baste all layers together.

2. Refer to Quilting and Finishing on page 67 for finishing the quilt. See Wavy Parallel Line quilting, page 71, to quilt like the sample. Use the (9) 2-1/4" -wide raspberry batik strips (or 364" total length) for binding.

Wavy Parallel Lines Quilting Diagram

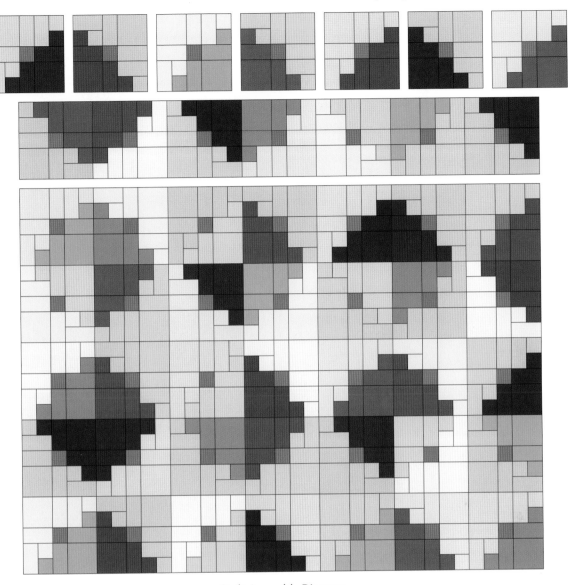

Quilt Assembly Diagram

Comfort

Less is more; that's the beauty of this quilt. Large analogue squares tipped with bright corner triangles make for a great first quilt project. This quilt has wool batting for loft and stitched-in-the-ditch by machine for a clean and simple finish.

UTILITY STYLE TIP

This is an easy quilt to make as large or as small as you want. For a different look, try this quilt with low-volume light squares and dark contrasting or bold-hued triangle corners. Randomly clustered placement of the large squares keeps this quilt from being predictable.

Finished Size: 48" x 56"

Finished Block 8" square

MATERIAL

2-7/8 yards total assorted blue, green, aqua, and gray solids

1 fat quarter light green solid

1 fat quarter coral solid

1/2 yard blue print for binding

3-1/4 yards backing

56" x 64" batting

Read through all instructions before beginning. Sew pieces right sides together and use a 1/4" seam allowance throughout unless otherwise stated.

CUTTING

From assorted blue, green, aqua, and gray solids, cut a total of:
(42) 8-1/2" squares

From each light green and coral fat quarter, cut:
(5) 2" x 21" strips then cut into (42) 2" squares.

From blue print, cut:
(6) 2-1/4" x 42" strips (or 220" total length) for binding.

BLOCK ASSEMBLY

1. Draw a diagonal line on the wrong side of each 2" square.

2. With right sides together, sew a 2" light green solid square on one corner of an 8-1/2" square, stitching on the drawn line. Trim 1/4" beyond the line, press the seam toward the 8-1/2" square. Repeat on the diagonally opposite corner with a marked 2" coral square to make a block. Make 42 blocks.

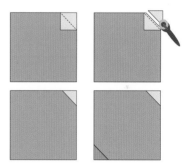

QUILT ASSEMBLY

1. Referring to the Quilt Assembly Diagram, page 44, and noting orientation, lay out blocks in 7 rows of 6 blocks each.

2. Join the blocks into rows. Join rows to complete quilt top.

FINISHING

1. Cut backing fabric into two 1-5/8 yard pieces. Cut selvages off and join together using a 1/2" seam allowance. Press seam and trim to 56" x 64". Layer the backing, batting and quilt top. Baste all layers together.

2. Refer to Quilting and Finishing on page 67 for finishing the quilt. See Stitch-in-the-Ditch quilting, page 70, to quilt like the sample. Use the (6) 2-1/4"-wide blue strips (or 220" total length) for binding.

STITCH-IN-THE-DITCH
Following the seam lines is one of the easiest methods of quilting and does not require any marking. Stitching on or very close to the seam line is how this stitch-in-the-ditch quilting method got it's name. Where seams have been pressed to one side, stitch along the seam on the three-layer side rather than the bulky, five-layer seam allowance side.

Use a regular presser foot or walking foot attachment for all straight-line quilting designs. You can start from the center and work outward like in the method of basting or you can start from one end and work straight through to the opposite side. Read more about stitching in the ditch and straight line quilting on page 70.

Quilt Assembly Diagram

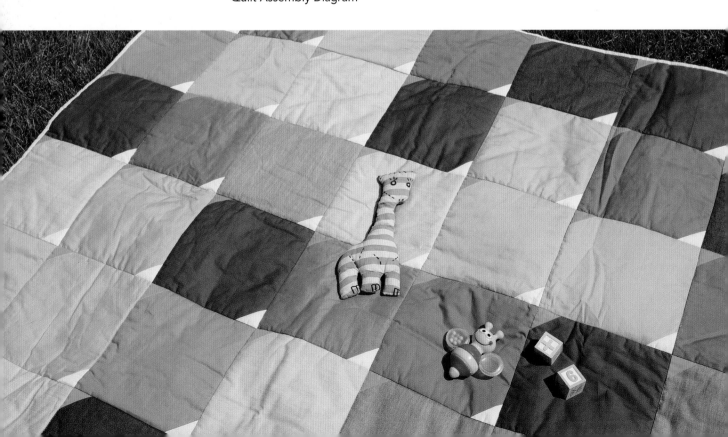

FABRIC AND QUILT CARE

Protect your investment by selecting patchwork appropriate materials from the start of your project, then assure your quilts a long life with proper cleaning and storage.

WASHING FABRIC

Typically patchwork quilts are made from 100% quilting cotton. Using materials of other fiber content and weights can lead to different degrees of shrinkage when washing, bulky seams, and uneven rate of wear.

Whether or not to pre-wash fabric for patchwork is a constant debate among quilters. Usually, I do not pre-wash my materials because I prefer how the fabric handles with the factory sizing in it. However, if using fabric that might shrink or transfer color later when I launder the quilt, I wash the material before cutting. If the fabric is vintage or from a thrift shop (like clothing), I launder to make sure it's fresh and sturdy enough for use in a quilt. Fabric subjected to sunlight and harsh temperatures can degrade over time and become brittle. Only use fabrics that are stable and strong enough for use in quilts.

QUILT CARE

Cleaning

Utility quilts are meant to be used, which inevitably means laundering.

I machine wash on a delicate cycle and use a gentle detergent such as Woolite. There are many quilt specific laundry products available on the market. Read the instructions on all products carefully. Set the machine temperature to cold for the wash and rinse and use a couple sheets of a color catching product to avoid any problems with bleeding and/or color transfer.

Air dry or dry your quilt on the lowest heat level available. Ideally, your quilt will not be completely dried but slightly damp. Finish by line-drying. Warm iron if desired.

Storage

If possible, store quilts flat (like on a bed) or rolled (like a carpet) to prevent creases or uneven wear. If you must store a quilt folded, add acid-free tissue cushions under the folds and refold frequently to redistribute the fold lines across the quilt.

The materials in a quilt are highly susceptible to the ravages of climate conditions such as dampness, excessive heat, and sunlight. Prolonged moisture can cause mold and stains. Excessive heat and exposure to sunlight can fade and break down cotton fibers.

Quilts exposed to sunlight will fade even if used on a bed. Blocking the amount of light a quilt receives will slow fading and rotating its orientation on the bed will result in more even fading.

Never store quilts in plastic bags. The non-porous properties of plastic will not allow moisture to escape or the fibers of the quilt breathability. A ridged plastic storage container is acceptable as long as it's stored in a dry environment.

Utility-Style Quilts for Everyday Living

Midsommar

Midsommar is a free-form quilt design that offers a wonderful opportunity to use leftover strips. Don't worry if your strips aren't long enough; you can combine fabrics to make the necessary length.

UTILITY STYLE TIP

With large expanses of fabrics, this quilt is a great way to showcase some of your favorite prints. Being careful not to throw everything in at once, use some solids or blenders, change up the scale of the prints and play with contrast to keep the vertical impact of this design apparent.

Finished Size: 72" x 80"

MATERIAL

1-1/4 yard white solid

1-1/4 yard purple floral

3/4 yard blue with dots

3/4 yard navy floral

1/2 yard yellow solid

1/2 yard lavender solid

5/8 yard stripe

5/8 yard yellow floral

1 fat quarter blue multi floral

8-1/2" square tiny purple floral

5/8 yard for binding

5 yards backing

80" x 88" batting

Read through all instructions before beginning. Sew pieces right sides together and use a 1/4" seam allowance throughout unless otherwise stated.

CUTTING

From white solid, cut:
(3) 8-1/2" x 42" strips.
Sew strips end-to-end to make one long strip.
Press, then cut:
   (2) 8-1/2" x 56-1/2" strips.

(2) 4-1/2" x 42" strips.
Sew strips end-to-end to make one long strip.
Press, then cut:
   (1) 4-1/2" x 56-1/2" strip,
   (1) 4-1/2" x 12-1/2" strip.

From purple floral, cut:
(4) 8-1/2" x 42" strips.
Sew strips end-to-end to make one long strip.
Press, then cut:
   (2) 8-1/2" x 56-1/2" strips,
   (1) 8-1/2" x 48-1/2" strip.

From blue dot, cut:
(2) 12-1/2" x 42" strips.
Sew strips end-to-end to make one long strip.
Press, then cut:
   (1) 12-1/2" x 72-1/2" strip.

From navy floral, cut:
(3) 8-1/2" x 42" strips.
Sew strips end-to-end to make one long strip.
Press, then cut:
   (1) 8-1/2" x 56-1/2" strip,
   (2) 8-1/2" x 12-1/2" rectangles,
   (1) 4-1/2" x 12-1/2" strip.

From yellow solid, cut:
(3) 4-1/2" x 42" strips.
Sew strips end-to-end to make one long strip.
Press, then cut:
   (1) 4-1/2" x 56-1/2" strip,
   (2) 4-1/2" x 12-1/2" strips,
   (1) 4-1/2" x 8-1/2" rectangle.

From lavender solid, cut:
(3) 4-1/2" x 42" strips.
Sew strips end-to-end to make one long strip.
Press, then cut:
    (1) 4-1/2" x 56-1/2" strip,
    (2) 4-1/2" x 12-1/2" strips.

From stripe, cut:
(1) 8-1/2" x 42" strip. From strip cut:
    (2) 8-1/2" x 12-1/2" rectangles.

(2) 4-1/2" x 42" strips.
Sew strips end-to-end to make one long strip.
Press, then cut:
    (1) 4-1/2" x 52-1/2" strip,
    (2) 4-1/2" x 12-1/2" strips.

From yellow floral, cut:
(1) 8-1/2" x 42" strip then cut into:
    (2) 8-1/2" x 12-1/2" rectangle.

(2) 4-1/2" x 42" strips.
Sew strips end-to-end to make one long strip.
Press, then cut:
    (1) 4-1/2" x 56-1/2" strip,
    (1) 4-1/2" square.

From blue multi floral, cut:
(2) 4-1/2" x 12-1/2" strips.

From binding fabric, cut:
(8) 2-1/4" x 42" strips (or 316" total length).

QUILT ASSEMBLY

1. Stitch (2) 4-1/2" x 12-1/2" yellow solid strips, (1) 4-1/2" x 12-1/2" stripe strip, (1) 4-1/2" x 12-1/2" blue multi floral strip and (1) 4-1/2" x 8-1/2" yellow solid rectangle together end-to-end, as shown.

2. Stitch (1) 4-1/2" x 52-1/2" stripe strip and (1) 4-1/2" yellow floral square together as shown.

3. Stitch (1) 8-1/2" x 48-1/2" purple floral strip and (1) 8-1/2" tiny purple floral square together as shown.

4. Referring to the Quilt Assembly Diagram, page 49, and noting placement, arrange the 56-1/2" long strips into 12 vertical rows as shown, alternating the 4-1/2" and 8-1/2" wide strips. Join rows to make section A. In the same manner, join the (12) 12-1/2" long strips and rectangles, alternating the widths to make section C.

5. Stitch the 12-1/2" x 72-1/2" blue dot strip (section B) between section A section C.

FINISHING

1. Cut backing fabric into two 2-1/2 yard pieces. Cut selvages off and join together lengthwise using a 1/2" seam allowance. Press seam open and trim to 80" x 90". Layer the backing, batting and quilt top. Baste all layers together.

2. Refer to Quilting and Finishing on page 67 for finishing the quilt. See Fan Pattern on page 71 to quilt like sample. Use the (8) 2-1/4"-wide strips (or 316" total length) for binding.

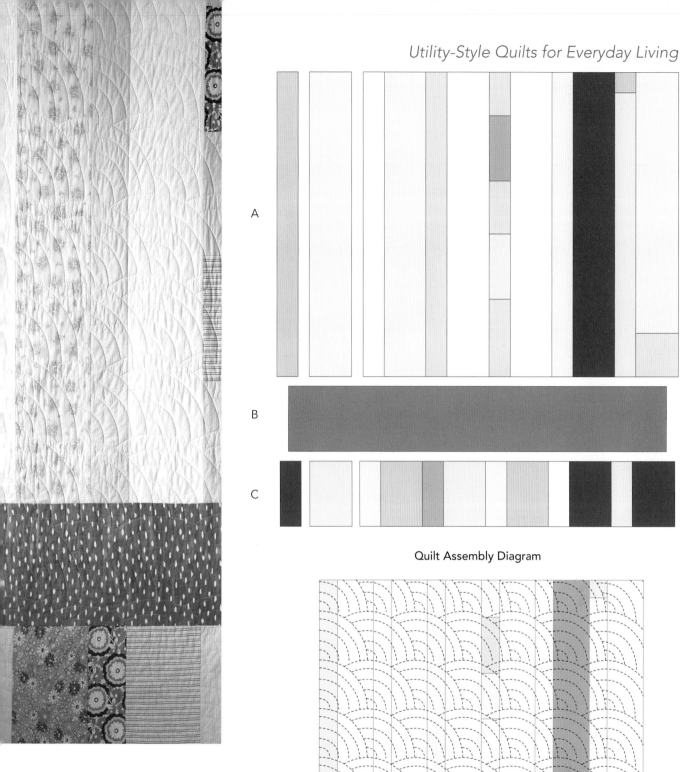

A

B

C

Quilt Assembly Diagram

Fan Quilting Diagram

REPEAT QUILT PATTERNS

Repeating quilt patterns provides an additional overall texture to the quilt. This type of quilt design needs to be drawn onto the quilt top before basting. Use the marking tool as instructed. Marking out a top is labor intensive but the time spent will be made up when quilting directly onto the markings.

Refer to Quilting on page 71 for stitching the Fan Pattern utility quilt design used on the *Midsommar* quilt.

Star Crossed

Playful patchwork blocks are set in wide scrappy sashing, making the quilt look as if it was made from limited fabric supplies.

UTILITY STYLE TIP
Intentionally pulling fabric selections with limited yardage makes creative substitutions a necessity. Choose similarly saturated replacement fabrics for unity.

Finished Size: 84" x 90"

Finished Block: 15" square

MATERIAL
1 fat quarter **each** of 12 assorted medium/dark fabric (or 2-1/2 yards total)

1-1/2 yards light peach solid for blocks and borders

1-1/2 yards dark pink solid for sashing

1 yard light print A for sashing and blocks

2/3 yard light print B for sashing

1/2 yard large plaid for borders

1-1/4 yards white solid for blocks

5/8 yard for binding

7-1/2 yards backing

92" x 98" batting

Read through all instructions before beginning. Sew pieces right sides together and use a 1/4" seam allowance throughout unless otherwise stated.

CUTTING
From the 12 assorted medium/dark fabrics, cut:
16 sets of 4 matching 3-7/8" squares
(for a total of 64 squares).

4 sets of 4 matching 3-1/2" x 6-1/2" rectangles
(for a total of 16 rectangles).

(80) assorted 3-1/2" squares.

From the light peach solid, cut:
(13) 3-1/2" x 42" strips. From 8 strips cut:
(48) 3-1/2" x 6-1/2" rectangles
(reserve remaining strips for borders)

From the dark pink solid, cut:
(7) 6-1/2" x 42" strips. From 3 strips cut:
(6) 6-1/2" x 15-1/2" strips
(reserve remaining strips for sashing).

From light print A, cut:
(4) 6-1/2" x 42" strips. From 2 strips cut:
(4) 6-1/2" x 15-1/2" strips
(reserve remaining strips for sashing).

(1) 3-7/8" x 42" strip. From strip cut:
(8) 3-7/8" squares.

(1) 3-1/2" x 42" strip. From strip cut:
(8) 3-1/2" squares.

From light print B, cut:
(3) 6-1/2" x 42" strips. From 1 strips cut:
(2) 6-1/2" x 15-1/2" strips
(reserve remaining strips for sashing).

From the large plaid, cut:
(2) 6-1/2" x 42" strips for sashing.

From the white solid, cut:
(6) 3-7/8" x 42" strips. From strips cut:
(56) 3-7/8" squares.

(5) 3-1/2" x 42" strips. From strips cut:
(56) 3-1/2" squares.

From the binding, cut:
(9) 2-1/4" x 42" strips (or 360" total length).

BLOCK ASSEMBLY

1. Draw a diagonal line on the wrong side of each 3-7/8" white solid and light print squares. Place a marked square right sides together with a 3-7/8" assorted medium/dark or solid square. Sew a 1/4" seam on each side of the line. Cut apart on the line. Press seam toward the medium/dark fabric. Trim dog ears. Make (2) 3-1/2" half-square triangle units. Make a total of 8 half-square triangle units.

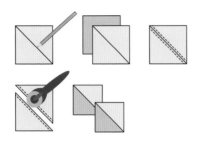

2. Noting placement and orientation, sew (1) 3-1/2" white solid or light print A square to a half-square triangle unit. Press toward the square. In the same manner, sew a half-square triangle unit to (1) 3-1/2" assorted medium/dark or solid square. Press toward the square. Join the rows to make a four-patch unit. Make a total of 4 four-patch units.

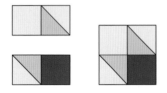

3. Arrange (4) 3-1/2" x 6-1/2" matching rectangles and (1) 3-1/2" medium/dark or solid square with 4 four-patch units as shown. Sew into rows. Join the rows to make 1 block. Make a total of 16 blocks.

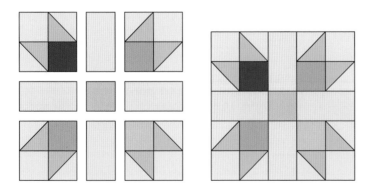

QUILT ASSEMBLY

1. Referring to the Quilt Assembly Diagram on page 53, sew (3) 6-1/2" x 15-1/2" sashing strips between 4 blocks to make a horizontal row. Make 4 horizontal rows.

2. Sew the 6-1/2" x 42" strips end-to-end to make one long strip. Note: The sashing for the sample quilt was made by sewing matching solids and prints in tandem, which adds a scrappier look to the quilt and staggers the placement of seams on the sashes. Press seams open to reduce bulk.

3. Measure the length of each block row. Average those numbers and cut 5 strips to this measurement from the long strip in Step 2. Join 3 strips between the block rows. Add a strip to each end for the top and bottom border.

4. Join the (5) 3-1/2" x 42" light peach solid strips end-to-end to make one long strip. Measure the length of the quilt. Cut 2 light peach solid strips to the measurement for side borders. Stitch to the sides of the quilt.

FINISHING

1. Cut backing fabric into three 2-1/2 yard pieces. Cut selvages off and join together lengthwise using a 1/2" seam allowance. Press seam open and trim to 92" x 98". Layer the backing, batting and quilt top. Baste all layers together.

2. Refer to Quilting and Finishing on page 67 for finishing the quilt. See Double-Line Crosshatch quilting to quilt like the sample. Use the (9) 2-1/4" -wide strips (or 360" total length) for binding.

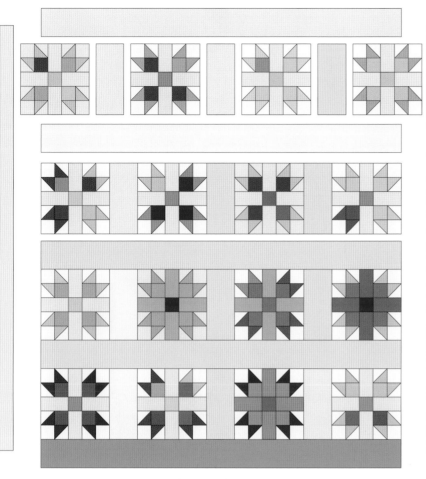

Quilt Assembly Diagram

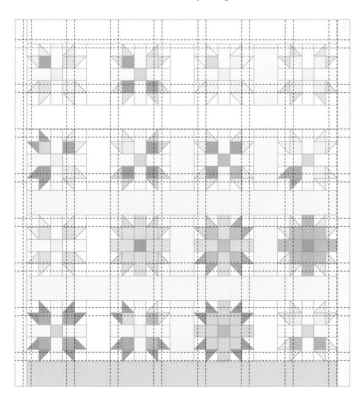

Double-Line Crosshatch Diagram

DOUBLE-LINE CROSSHATCH QUILTING

Whether stitched in one direction or on the diagonal, parallel straight lines can all be created with continuous line quilting. Marking or masking out stitch lines prior to quilting can be helpful if not following seam lines. Parallel lines can be evenly or randomly spaced. A double-line crosshatch has two parallel lines instead of one to create a plaid effect Read more about how this quilt was quilted on page 71.

Bobbin

Bobbin is based on an unassuming nine-patch arrangement patchwork block which, when set together in rows, creates a lovely secondary design.

....

UTILITY STYLE TIP
Contrasting fabrics make this block shine. The design could be stunning as a two-color quilt. Experiment with random or orderly block placement, or a mixture of both like in the sample quilt. A few low-volume blocks were deliberately included to almost fade away from the rest of the quilt creating an off-balance feel to what might have been a symmetrical layout.

Finished Size: 72" square

Finished Block 12" square

MATERIAL
1/2 yard dark blue solid

1/2 yard turquoise solid

1/2 yard white solid

1/3 yard olive solid

1/3 yard aqua solid

1/3 yard teal solid

7/8 yard coral solid
(includes binding)

5/8 yard **each** 6 light prints

3/4 yard light print

4-1/2 yards backing

80" square batting

Read through all instructions before beginning. Sew pieces right sides together and use a 1/4" seam allowance throughout unless otherwise stated.

CUTTING
From each of dark blue, turquoise, and white solid, cut:
(3) 4-7/8" x 42" strips. From strips cut:
    (18) 4-7/8" squares

From each of olive and aqua solid, cut:
(2) 4-7/8" x 42" strips. From strips cut:
    (15) 4-7/8" squares.

From the teal solid, cut:
(2) 4-7/8" x 42" strips. From strips cut:
    (12) 4-7/8" squares.

From the coral solid, cut:
(2) 4-7/8" x 42" strips. From strips cut:
    (12) 4-7/8" squares.

(7) 2-1/4" x 42" strips for binding (294" total length)

From each of the (6) 5/8 yard light prints, cut:
(2) 4-7/8" x 42" strips. From strips cut:
    (15) 4-7/8" squares.

(2) 4-1/2" x 42" strips. From strips cut:
    (15) 4-1/2" squares.

From the 3/4 yard light print, cut:
(3) 4-7/8" x 42" strips. From strips cut:
    (18) 4-7/8" squares.

(2) 4-1/2" x 42" strips. From strips cut:
    (18) 4-1/2" squares.

BLOCK ASSEMBLY
1. Draw a diagonal line on the wrong side of a 4-7/8" light print square. Place the square, right sides together, on top of a 4-7/8" solid square. Sew a 1/4" seam allowance on each side of the line. Cut apart on line. Press seams toward the solid. Trim dog ears. Makes (2) 4-1/2" half-square triangle units. Make a total of 6 matching half-square triangle units. See illustrations on page 56.

2. Refer to Quilting and Finishing on page 67 to finish the quilt. Sample was quilted in a Diagonal Crosshatch quilting pattern, page 70. Use the (7) 2-1/4"-wide coral solid strips (or 294" total length) for binding.

Diagonal Crosshatch Quilting Diagram

2. Noting placement and orientation, arrange 6 matching half-square triangle units and (3) 4-1/2" matching light print squares as shown. Stitch into rows. Join rows to make a block. Make 36 blocks.

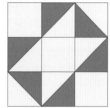

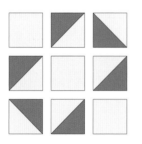

QUILT ASSEMBLY
1. Referring to Quilt Assembly Diagram on page 57, and noting placement and orientation, arrange blocks in 6 rows of 6 blocks.

2. Join the blocks into rows. Join rows together to complete quilt top.

FINISHING
1. Cut backing fabric into two 2-1/4 yard pieces. Cut selvages off and join together lengthwise using a 1/2" seam allowance. Press seam open and trim to 80" square. Layer the backing, batting and quilt top. Baste all layers together.

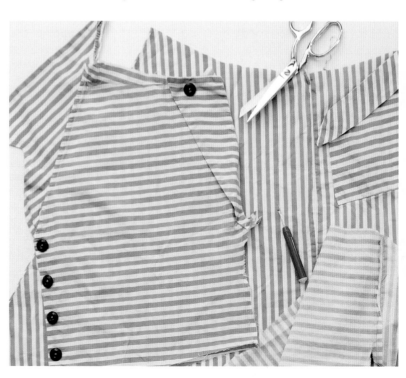

Repurposing garments for use in quilts is fun and economical

Quilt Assembly Diagram

Sunday Paper

Sometimes you just want to go big! Sunday Paper uses 36" blocks to make piecing fast. With fewer seams and larger areas of fabric, this pattern is perfect for showing off utility-style quilting designs.

UTILITY STYLE TIP

This quilt can be made so many ways. Flip the focus by making the background dark and the starts light. Make it as scrappy as you like or stitch a classic two- or three-color quilt. Or lower the amount of contrast by choosing fabric of closer value to de-emphasize the stars.

Finished Size: 72" square

Finished Block: 36" square

MATERIAL

1 yard **each** 4 assorted light prints (or 4 yards total) for background

1/3 yard **each** 10 assorted medium/dark fabrics (or 3-1/3 yards total)

5/8 yard for binding

4-1/2 yards backing

80" square batting

Read through all instructions before beginning. Sew pieces right sides together and use a 1/4" seam allowance throughout unless otherwise stated.

CUTTING

From each of the 4 assorted light prints, cut:
(2) 9-7/8" x 42" strips. From strips, cut:
   (6) 9-7/8" squares.

(1) 9-1/2" x 42" strip. From strip cut:
   (4) 9-1/2" squares.

From the 10 assorted medium/dark fabrics, cut:
(16) assorted 10-1/4" squares,
(8) assorted 9-7/8" squares.

From binding fabric, cut:
(8) 2-1/4" x 42" strips (or 300" total length).

BLOCK ASSEMBLY

1. Select 2 different 10-1/4" medium/dark squares. Draw a diagonal line on the wrong side of the lighter square. Place squares right sides together and sew a 1/4" seam on each side of the drawn line. Cut apart on the line. Press seams toward darker print. Trim dog ears. Makes (2) 9-7/8" half-square triangle units. Make 4 half-square triangle units.

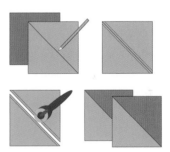

2. Draw a diagonal line on the wrong side of (1) 9-7/8" light print square. Place marked light print square right sides together with a half-square triangle unit from Step 1. Draw a diagonal line, perpendicular to the seam line on the wrong side of the half-square triangle unit. Stitch a 1/4" seam on each side of the marked line. Cut apart on line. Press seams open to reduce bulk. Trim dog ears. Makes (2) 9-1/2" three-triangle units. Repeat for remaining half-square triangle units using different 9-7/8" light print squares. Make a total of (8) three-triangle units. Set aside.

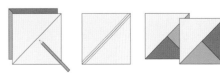

3. Select a 9-7/8" light print square and a 9-7/8" medium/dark square. Draw a diagonal line on the

wrong side of the light square. In the same manner as in Step 1, make (2) 9-1/2" half-square triangle units. Press seams open and trim dog ears. Make 4 half-square triangle units.

4. Arrange (4) 9-1/2" light print squares, (8) 3-triangle units, and 4 half-square triangle units as shown. Sew into 4 rows. Join rows to make a block. Make 4 blocks.

quilting to quilt like the *Sunday Paper* sample. Use the (8) 2-1/4"-wide strips (or 300" total length) for binding.

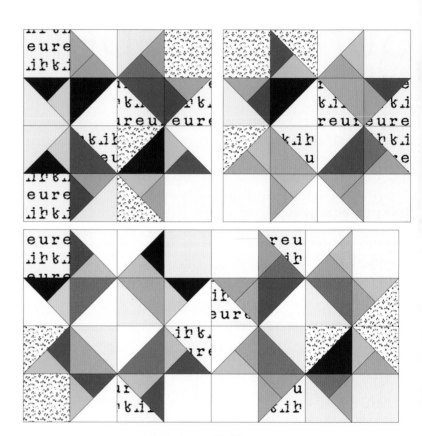

Quilt Assembly Diagram

QUILT ASSEMBLY
1. Referring to Quilt Assembly Diagram, arrange blocks in 2 rows of 2 blocks each, as shown.

2. Join the blocks into rows. Join rows together to complete quilt top.

FINISHING
1. Cut backing fabric into two 2-1/4 yard pieces. Cut selvages off and join together lengthwise, using a 1/2" seam allowance. Press seam open and trim to 80" square. Layer the backing, batting and quilt top. Baste all layers together.

2. Refer to Quilting and Finishing on page 67 for finishing the quilt. See Parallel Diagonal

Parallel Diagonal Quilting Diagram

Goose Chase

With economy of fabric in mind, the bias binding for this quilt is made using the leftover halves of the center triangles.

UTILITY STYLE TIP
Ten different fabrics were used for the sample, but this project could easily be sewn with a scrappier look. Big patchwork pieces are a great place to use some large-scale prints. If you're new to quilting, using patterned fabric in the central half-square triangle area will camouflage any unsteady quilting stitches.

Finished Size: 56" square

MATERIAL
7/8 yard dark peach solid
(includes binding)

7/8 yard pink solid
(includes binding)

1 yard olive solid

1/4 yard aqua print

1/4 yard gray print

1/4 yard light print

1/4 yard large floral

1/4 yard mauve solid

1/4 yard off-white stripe

1/4 yard blue geometric

3-5/8 yards backing

64" square batting

Read through all instructions before beginning. Sew pieces right sides together and use a 1/4" seam allowance throughout unless otherwise stated.

CUTTING
From each of the dark peach and pink solid, cut:
(1) 29" square,
(2) 7-7/8" squares.

From the olive solid, cut:
(1) 14-1/2" x 42" strip. From strip cut:
   (2) 14-1/2" squares.

(2) 7-7/8" x 42" strips. From strips, cut:
   (10) 7-7/8" squares.

From each of the aqua, gray, and light prints, cut:
(1) 7-7/8" x 42" strip. From strip cut:
   (5) 7-7/8" squares.

From each of the mauve solid and off-white stripe, cut:
(1) 7-7/8" x 42" strip. From strip cut:
   (3) 7-7/8" squares.

From blue geometric, cut:
   (2) 7-7/8" squares.

FLYING GEESE ASSEMBLY
1. Referring to the Pairing Diagram, pair the 7-7/8" squares to make a total of 21 pairs.

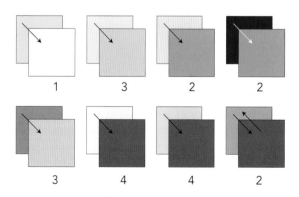

1   3   2   2

3   4   4   2

Pairing Diagram

2. Draw a diagonal line on the wrong side of the lighter fabric in each pair. Place right sides together with it's 7-7/8" square pairing. Sew a 1/4" seam on each side of the drawn line. Cut apart on line. Press seams in direction indicated by arrows on the Pairing Diagram.

Note: Press half the olive/dark peach solid HSTs toward the olive side and half toward the dark peach side. Trim dog ears. Make a total of (42) 7-1/2" half-square triangle units. (Note: There will be two unused half-square triangles.)

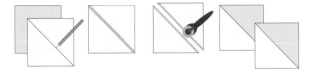

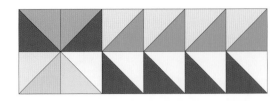

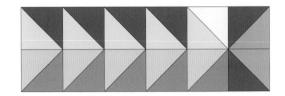

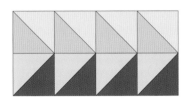

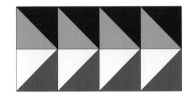

Section Assembly Diagram

3. Refer to the Flying Geese Diagram and noting orientation, sew the HST units into flying geese units. Make a total of 20 flying geese.

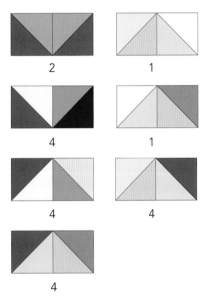

Flying Geese Diagram

QUILT ASSEMBLY

1. Draw a straight line with marking tool and ruler diagonally from corner to corner on the 29" dark peach solid square. Cut on the drawn line and set one half-square triangle aside for binding. Repeat with the 29" pink square.

2. Sew the dark peach and light pink large half-square triangles together on the diagonal edge, being careful not to stretch the bias edge. Using a ruler and rotary cutter, square the half-square triangle unit to 28-1/2" square.

3. Stitch the Flying Geese blocks into sections as shown in the Section Assembly Diagram.

4. Referring to the Quilt Assembly Diagram on page 65 and noting placement and orientation, arrange the Flying Geese sections, 14-1/2" olive squares, and large dark peach and pink solid half-square triangles as shown. Sew into 3 horizontal rows. Join rows to complete quilt top.

BIAS BINDING

1. Refer to Bias Binding on page 74. From remaining large dark peach triangle, and working from the diagonal cut edge, mark parallel lines every 2-1/4".

2. Cut on drawn lines to make bias binding strips. Place 2 strips right sides together. Sew on the short ends with a 1/4" seam allowance. Press seams open. Continue adding strips to make one long bias strip.

3. With remaining large pink triangle, and working from the diagonal cut edge, mark parallel lines every 2-1/4". Cut on drawn lines to make bias binding strips.

4. Continue adding pink strips to the dark peach bias binding strip, pressing seams open. Trim off dog ears. Fold binding in half lengthwise with wrong sides together and press.

FINISHING

1. Cut backing fabric into two 1-7/8 yard pieces. Cut selvages off and join together, using a 1/2" seam allowance. Press seam open and trim to 64" square. Layer the backing, batting and quilt top. Baste all layers together.

2. Refer to Quilting and Finishing on page 67 for finishing the quilt. Use the prepared two-tone, 2-1/4"-wide bias binding (or 236" total length) to finish the quilt.

VARIED PARALLEL LINE QUILTING

Whether stitched in one direction or on the diagonal, parallel straight lines can all be created with continuous line quilting. Marking or masking out stitch lines prior to quilting can be helpful if not following seam lines. Parallel lines can be evenly or randomly spaced. Read more about how this quilt was quilted on page 70.

Quilt Assembly Diagram

Varied Parallel Line Quilting Diagram

QUILTING AND FINISHING

A quilt is not finished until it has a top, batting, and backing that are held together with stitching. Finishing a quilt requires a few additional supplies.

BATTING

Batting comprises the middle layer of a quilt. It comes in a variety of sizes and fiber content. Knowing how your quilt will be used and how close or far apart you intend to quilt or tie your quilt aids in selecting the best batting for your project. Manufacturer's labels include fiber content, construction, loft, distance between quilting, ease of use for different quilting applications (hand or machine), and washing care and shrinkage.

Synthetic fibers are lightweight and have a soft drape. They are available in a variety of lofts, add warmth, don't shrink, and are crease-resistant. Synthetic batting withstands years of use and is hypoallergenic, making it ideal for those with allergies.

Natural and renewable fibers offer breathability. Subject to shrink with the first washing, natural fibers will get softer with each wash. Cotton batting is low-loft and easy to baste because the cotton fabric clings to the batting. It can be heavy in large quilts and have a flat drape, and it is prone to creasing. Wool batting is warm and has a medium loft, which brings more definition to the quilting stitches. It is also crease-resistant.

Blended fiber batting is engineered to perform in a specific way by combining the strengths of natural and synthetic fibers. This creates a batting that is lightweight, soft, and crease resistant.

Needle-punched batting is a good choice when hand quilting because it allows the needle to pass through the fibers more easily. Scrim added to batting acts as a stabilizer, allowing for quilting stitches that are further apart and is a good choice when machine quilting. Bonded batting is a good choice for machine quilting but needs to be quilted denser than scrim coated batting.

ADDITIONAL QUILTING SUPPLIES

Spray Baste – This is optional and quilters, like myself, use spay baste to hold the sandwiched layers together for quilting or tying. Spray baste is a re-positional adhesive specially formulated for fabric to hold the layers in place. It requires adequate ventilation and a protective surface underneath when applied. The biggest advantage to spray basting is that it means no time-consuming pin basting and no stopping while quilting to remove any pins.

Curved Safety Pins – Pin basting can be time consuming but is a common way to secure the sandwiched layers for quilting or tying. Unlike spray baste, pins are reusable but they are much more labor intensive. They are a good choice for someone who wants to avoid fumes or adhesives. If pin basting, a closing tool like Kwik Klip may well be worth the investment.

Tape – I use duct tape for holding the backing in place on a hard surface when layering and basting the sandwiched layers. Painter's tape and/or specifically made quilting tape are handy for marking straight-line quilting guides and come in a variety of widths. Note: Remove tape guides promptly as they may leave a sticky residue on the fabric if left for long periods.

Marking Tool – Carefully read the manufacturer's instructions before choosing a marking tool. Some markings can become permanent if used incorrectly.

NEEDLES

Long hand-sewing needles are good for thread basting a quilt sandwich.

Larger eye needles are used for heavier thread and tying a quilt to make a comforter.

Between needles are small-eyed, sharp needles for hand quilting.

Sharps are needles for hand-piecing, appliqué, and hand sewing binding to the back of a quilt.

Curved needles are helpful for easier thread basting.

Thimble – Thimbles protect your finger(s) when hand stitching and make it easier to push a needle through the layers of a quilt top.

Quilting frame or hoop – A quilting frame or hoop comes in a variety of sizes and holds the layers of a quilt taut during hand quilting.

Binder Clip – Office supply binder clips, metal hair clips, or specialty sewing clips are handy for holding binding in place when hand or machine stitching to the back of a quilt.

MAKING THE QUILT SANDWICH

A quilt consists of three layers: the quilt top, the batting, and the backing. These layers are sandwiched, wrong sides together, and basted together for finishing.

Cut and piece the backing 4" beyond all edges of your quilt top, or at least 8" larger then the measurements of the quilt top, using a 1/2" seam allowance. Press the seam(s) open to reduce bulk. Press the quilt top and backing well.

If using the services of a longarm quilter, ask them for their preferred backing size. Press your quilt top and backing well and keep the layers separate.

Note: Marking the quilt top before layering the quilt sandwich is suggested for stenciled and detailed, planned quilt designs. Tape the pressed quilt top, right side up on a hard, flat surface while marking.

Layer the backing wrong side up on the flat surface and tape the edges of the backing fabric to the surface. The backing should be smooth but not stretched tight when taping down.

Layer the batting, cut to the same size with edges matching the backing.

If spray basting the layers, follow the manufacturer's instructions on the product. Fold back half of the batting onto itself. Working from the center and parallel with the fold of the batting, spray sections of the backing one at a time and smooth the batting in place. Repeat for the other half.

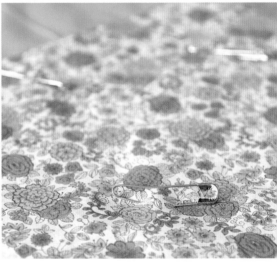

Position the quilt top, centered, right side up over batting. If pinning or thread basting, proceed to Pinning or Thread Basting. If spray basting, repeat for adhering the quilt top by spraying the batting in sections and smoothing the top in place as you work. Remove tape from the edges of the backing.

PINNING OR THREAD BASTING
Beginning in the center, insert an open safety pin through all three layers of the quilt sandwich. Close the safety pin.

Continue placing safety pins, smoothing the quilt top as pins are added. Place pins approximately 4" apart, using your fist as a guide. Tip: If you will be machine quilting, place the pins away from the lines to be quilted.

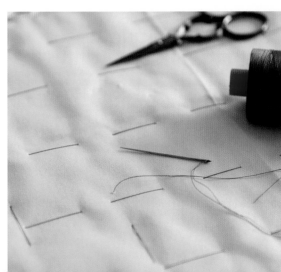

To thread baste, start in the center of the quilt. Use a contrasting or easily seen thread color to make approximately 2" long stitches through all layers. Space stitches 3"-4" apart across the quilt surface, stitching in a vertical and horizontal grid pattern.

MACHINE QUILTING

Quilting your quilt using a sewing machine can be fun and rewarding. Beginners may want to practice on a scrap quilt sandwich or small projects before tackling larger, bulky quilts. There are two types of machine quilting attachments available to quilter's that produce different results.

Walking-Foot - or "even-feed foot" moves the layers of the quilt through the sewing machine evenly. This is the best choice for straight-line quilting and stitch-in-the-ditch quilting applications. See Utility Quilting on page 67.

Darning - or "free-motion foot" is used while the machine feed dogs are dropped and allows the quilter to move the fabric across the throat plate in any direction. It is best used for meandering, fan or wave designs, and organic quilting (see Utility Quilting on page 67).

Beginning quilters may want to choose a thread color that blends with the majority of the colors in their quilt until they feel more confident about their machine quilting abilities. Select a quality 40- or 50-weight thread of 100% cotton or a poly-cotton blend.

Be sure to consider the spacing requirements of your batting when deciding on your quilt design. Different batting fibers require various quilting densities for best performance. See Batting on page 67.

With ample backing and batting around the centered quilt top and a properly basted quilt sandwich, there's no need to start quilting in the center. In fact, some utility quilting designs work best starting from one corner and working the stitches in rows. All of the quilting designs in this book can be used for either machine or hand quilting. See page 33 for Hand Quilting.

1. Place the quilt sandwich under the presser foot where you want to begin quilting. Hold the top thread in your left hand and lower the needle into the quilt. Lower the presser foot.

2. Take one stitch to pull the bobbin thread up. Hold top and bobbin thread while sewing the first few stitches, taking a backstitch or two to secure the stitches. Carefully trim thread ends close to quilt surface.

3. Continue stitching, sewing with the needle in the down position, if available. Repeat Steps 1 and 2 each time you begin a new section or re-thread your machine. Tip: Continually stop and smooth out the quilt sandwich as you stitch, checking that the layers are flat. You may want to roll the areas not being sewn to reduce bulk around the sewing area, making it easier to handle and move through the machine.

UTILITY QUILTING

The simplicity of utility quilts being easy to make carries through to the finishing. Utility quilting is a simple, overall stitching that generally pays little heed to the quilt top design. Its purpose is to hold the layers together and its practicality is suited to continuous line quilting.

STRAIGHT LINE
Stitch-in-the-Ditch
Following the seam lines is one of the easiest methods of quilting and does not require any marking. Where seams have been pressed to one side, stitch along the seam on the three-layer side rather than the bulky, five-layer seam allowance side. See *Comfort* on page 42 for an example of a quilt finished with this stitch-in-the-ditch method.

Use a regular presser foot or walking foot attachment for all straight-line quilting designs. You can start from the center and work outward like in the method of basting or you can start from one end and work straight through to the opposite side.

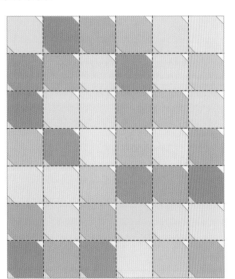

Stitch-in-the-Ditch Diagram

Referring to the Stitch-in-the-Ditch Diagram, quilt horizontal lines first. When you reach the end of the first line, leave the needle in the down position and pivot the quilt 45°. Without cutting the threads or removing the quilt from the machine, continue stitching 1/8" from the raw edge, parallel to the vertical side of the quilt until you meet the next horizontal seam line. Stop with the needle down, pivot the quilt 45°, and continue in the same manner. Repeat stopping, rotating, and stitching until all the horizontal stitch lines have been completed. Stitch the vertical seam lines in the same manner.

Parallel Straight Lines
Whether stitched in one direction (*Pixel and Viewpoint*), crosshatched (*Star Crossed* and *Comfort*), or on the diagonal (*Goose Chase, Bobbin,* and *Sunday Paper*), parallel straight lines can all be created with continuous line quilting. Marking or masking out stitch lines prior to quilting is helpful when not following seam lines. Parallel lines can be evenly or randomly spaced.

Quilt all the parallel lines in one direction first. When you reach the end of the first stitch line leave the needle in the down position and pivot the quilt 45°. Without cutting the threads or removing the quilt from the machine, continue stitching 1/8" from the raw edge, parallel to the vertical side of the quilt until you meet the next parallel seam line. Stop with the needle down, pivot the quilt 45°, and continue in the same manner. Repeat stopping, rotating, and stitching until all the stitch lines in that direction have been completed. If the quilt design calls for Crosshatch or Diagonal Crosshatch lines work the second parallel line direction in the same manner.

Parallel Diagonal
Refer to the Parallel Diagonal Diagram on page 71 for the following three utility-style quilting techniques. Parallel diagonal lines can be stitched in one direction across the quilt or subdivided into quarters and the parallel diagonal lines meet at the center like seen on *Sunday Paper* page 58.

Diagonal Crosshatch
Evenly spaced diagonal lines using the corners of the squares as guidelines for line placement. Stitch all one direction across the quilt top then repeat diagonally opposite to create crosshatch effect. See *Bobbin* page 54.

Varied Direction
Randomly placed parallel lines of quilting. This sort of design can be stitched in an improvisational manner, but I prefer to mark the entire quilt surface prior to stitching. See *Goose Chase* page 63.

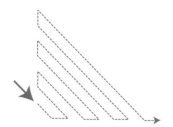

Parallel Diagonal Diagram

Double-Line Crosshatch

A double-line crosshatch has two parallel lines instead of one to create a plaid effect The example stitched on *Star Crossed* page 50 is made with vertical and horizontal lines.

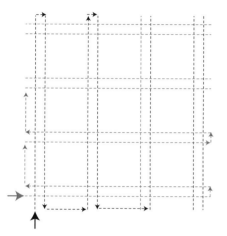

Double-Line Crosshatch Diagram

Wavy Parallel Lines

A darning foot should be used for organic shapes and wavy line quilting. With the machine feed dogs dropped the quilt can be moved under the needle freely and curves made more easily. Wavy parallel or wavy crosshatched designs are made in the same continuous manner as in straight-line quilting.

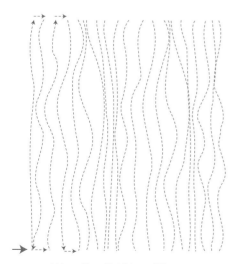

Wavy Parallel Lines Diagram

REPEAT QUILT PATTERNS

Repeating quilt patterns provide an additional overall texture to the quilt. This type of quilt design needs to be marked onto the quilt top before basting. Use the marking tool as instructed. Marking a quilt top is labor intensive but is time well spent.

Elbow Pattern

This pattern can be adjusted to whatever size you'd like, but to keep a continuous quilting line there must be an odd number of elbows in the repeat. Begin at a corner of the quilt to lay out the quilt pattern. For quilted example see *Cabin* on page 18.

Mark the smallest elbow section first by aligning a ruler with the side of the quilt. Establish the height and width of the smallest elbow noting it should be at least twice as tall as it is wide. Use the same width when spacing the next elbow marks. Make 4 more elbows, stepping out the shape as you go. Remember, you can make the elbow repeat larger, Just use an odd number of concentric elbows.

Repeat in the same manner, butting the next repeat up to the longest line of the first. Continue adding repeats to make a row. Additional rows are started on top, below, or to the side of the first depending upon where you started on your quilt or which direction you're working from. Don't worry if your design "falls off the edge", it will add to the utility quilt aesthetic.

Quilt the repeat pattern in the same way as it was marked, starting at the beginning of a row on the shortest line of the smallest elbow as shown. Use a presser foot or walking foot for this design. Each time you reach a corner, stop with the needle in the down position, pivot the quilt 45°, stitch to the next marked line, stop, pivot, and continue sewing to the end of the row. Note: The red arrows indicate bridge stitching and where you will need to trace stitch over earlier stitching to keep a continuous line flow to the quilting stitches. To start a new row, remove the quilt from the machine and begin the next row in the same manner and position as the first row.

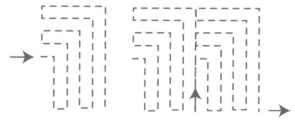

Elbow Pattern Diagram

Fan Pattern

Use a free-motion darning foot attachment for making this curved repeat quilt pattern. See *Midsommar* page 46 for an example of the fan pattern.

Use a non-permanent fabric-marking tool and follow manufacturers instructions for marking your quilt top. It doesn't hurt to test marks on scrap material to make sure they can be removed completely before proceeding. Determine how far apart you want the radiating fan arches.

Cut a 13" length of embroidery floss (light colored works best). Lay the floss out against a ruler and mark 6 evenly spaced segments starting about 1/2" from the end. Cut a 1/2" to 1" tail after the last mark. Slightly unscrew the tip of the marking tool and wind the floss around the marking tool tip just so the last mark is secured in the tip once tightened. If using a marking tool without a screw tip, use tape to hold the floss in place at the mark. Note: You may need to re-secure the floss as you work, just pay attention if your fan designs start to get a little out of shape. You now have an odd number of marks showing on your floss.

With the floss attached to the marking tool. Hold the first mark on the floss at a corner starting point on the quilt top. While holding the floss with one hand, mark an arch with the marking tool. Move the second mark on the floss to the corner starting point and make a smaller arch in the same manner as the first. Continue adding arches for a total of 5 concentric rings.

To add additional fans, repeat these steps, starting at the base of the large ring of the previous fan. Continue adding fans until the end of the row. Start the next row directly above your first row.

To quilt, begin at the small arch of the first row in the same manner in which the pattern was drawn. The red arrows indicate bridge stitching and where you will need to stitch over previously stitched lines to keep a

continuous flow to the quilting stitches. Each arch will be quilted the same direction till you reach the end of the row. Remove the quilt, and start at the beginning of the second row, quilting in the same direction as before.

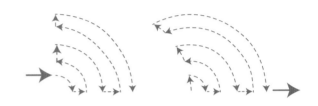

Remove the markings after quilting and binding, following the manufacturer's instructions for your marking tool. I then gently wash my new quilt in the washing machine. See Fabric and Quilt Care page 45.

Orange Peel
This repeating quilt pattern should be marked out before quilting as well.

Use a paper plate as a template. Fold the plate in half twice to divide the circle into quarters, crease folds. Beginning at one corner of the quilt and working in rows, mark the first circle.

Abut the next circle to the first, aligning the top and bottoms. Continue till the end of the row, not worrying if the last circle runs off the edge of the quilt top. Start a second row directly above the first with edges touching.

Using the quarter circle crease lines, align the third row a half circle over and centered between the first two rows of circles. Tip: To help with placement and alignment you may want to make additional tiny marks on the quilt surface where the quarters of the circles intersect. Continue adding circles in the same manner to make a repeating Orange Peel pattern.

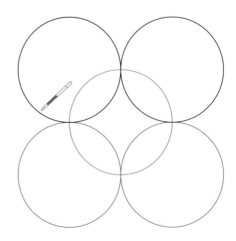

To quilt this pattern it's best not to think of this design as circles but rather as rows of scalloped half-circles as shown. Working vertically or horizontally across the top, complete one row of scallops, stop with the needle in the down position, rotate the quilt 45° and stitch parallel to the edge of the quilt to the next closest scallop. Stop, rotate the quilt, and begin sewing the next scallop row. Continue until the entire surface is quilted.

Feel free to experiment with variations on any of these utility quilting designs. Mix and match, make large or small, or include a few different styles in your quilt. There's no rules here other than selecting the proper quilt spacing for your batting type and preferred finishing method.

BINDING

Binding finishes the edges of a quilt, encasing the raw edges. The finished binding shows on the front and the back of the quilt. The double thickness of a binding edge makes a durable protective edge against wear and usage. The two most common types of binding are double-fold regular binding and double-fold bias binding.

Binding cut on the bias is more durable because the fibers run on a 45° angle to the cut strip, rather than across the strip. What that means is there are more layers of thread to wear through along the edge of the binding with bias-cut strips than with straight of grain binding. Bias binding also has stretch, which makes it the better choice for binding curved edges.

Binding is included in the project materials list as a specific number binding strips and as a total length in inches. Either option uses the same amount of fabric but the method for making them is different. Decide what type of binding you would like before cutting the binding strips.

DOUBLE-FOLD REGULAR BINDING

To make the double-fold binding place (2) 2-1/4" x width of fabric strips right sides together at right angles. Sew a diagonal seam. Continue adding strips in the same manner to make one long strip. Trim seams to 1/4". Press seams open. Proceed to Step 1 on Attaching the Binding.

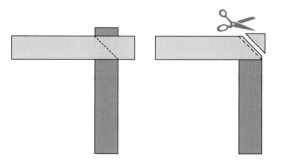

DOUBLE-FOLD BIAS BINDING

1. Remove selvage edges from fabric and cut into a square.

2. Fold the square diagonally, matching edges. Press the fold to form a crease line.

Open material. Use the fold line as the starting line and draw a line with pencil and ruler diagonally from corner to corner. Working in one direction from the center marked line, draw parallel lines 2-1/4" apart. Repeat on the opposite side of the center fold line. Cut strips on drawn lines.

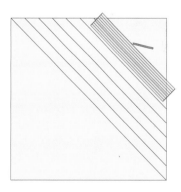

3. Referring to the illustration in Step 1 of Double fold Regular Binding, place two strips, right sides together. Sew with a 1/4" seam allowance on the short edge. Continue adding strips together end-to-end to make one long strip. Proceed to Step 1 on Attaching the Binding.

ATTACHING THE BINDING

1. Fold the strip lengthwise in half with wrong sides together and press.

2. Starting at the center of one edge of the quilt and place the folded binding on the right side of the top with raw edges aligned. Start 12" in from the end and begin stitching with a 1/4" seam allowance. Sew to the corner and backstitch 1/4" from the edge. Remove the quilt from the machine. Fold the strip up at a 45° angle and then back down over itself, lining up the raw edges to make a mitered corner.

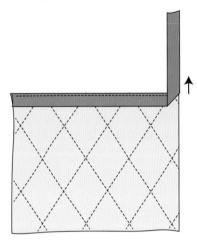

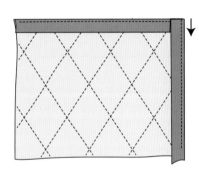

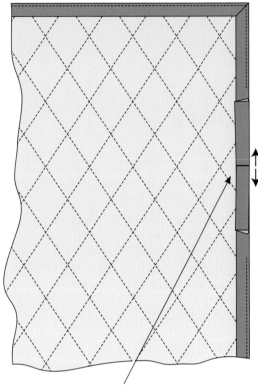

Fold binding ends back onto themselves with folded edges touching

3. Resume stitching, beginning at the top edge of the new side and continuing around the quilt to the next corner. Repeat Step 2, for remaining corners. Continue around the quilt to within 12" of the starting point. Backstitch. Remove the quilt from the machine.

5. Lay the quilt top on a flat surface. Bring the loose ends of the binding together so the binding and the quilt lay flat. Fold the binding ends back onto themselves so the folded edges touch but do not overlap. Finger press to crease. Open the binding. Place the strips at right angles, right sides together, using the creases to align the strips as indicated by arrows. Pin the ends together as shown. Draw a diagonal line from the corner intersections. Sew on the line. Before trimming the seam allowance refold the binding and check that it lays flat on the quilt top. Adjust the stitching if needed. Check and trim seam allowance to 1/4" when satisfied. Pin the binding down and sew the remaining section to the quilt top.

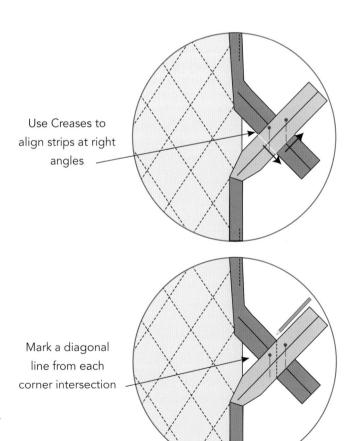

Use Creases to align strips at right angles

Mark a diagonal line from each corner intersection

6. Trim the backing and batting even with the quilt top.

7. Turn the binding to the back of the quilt, covering the stitch line. I use office supply binder clips to hold my binding in place (a section roughly 18" at a time) as I stitch it down.

8. Thread the needle with an 18" single strand of quality thread in a color that will blend in with the backing and binding. Knot the end of the thread.

9. Insert the knotted thread into the outer edge of the quilt to be hidden under the binding. Fold over a section of binding to the left of the starting stitch if right handed and to the right of the starting stitch if left handed. Secure the turned binding section with clips.

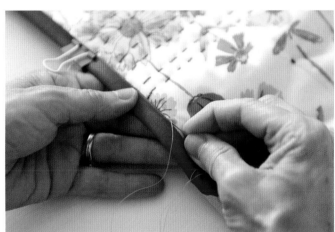

10. Begin slip stitching the binding to the back of the quilt with short, even stitches. Be sure not to sew through the quilt top layer. Stitch only through the edge of the folded binding, backing, and batting. Continue stitching and moving the clips as needed.

11. When you run out of thread, knot the end of the thread and bury the thread in the binding in the same manner as burying the thread when hand quilting. See page 33.

12. Fold a miter in the binding at the corners. Make a few concealed stitches into the miter fold to keep the corners flat and secure.

ACKNOWLEDGMENTS

Special thanks to the following families for allowing me into their homes for photography:

- The Collins Family

- Jessica, Ndiba, Jemea, and Diele Dioh

- Karen Meyer

- The Ruppert Family

Sincere gratitude to Susan Playsted for photographing her beautiful home for lifestyle inset photos. Proving once again just how amazing friendships can be formed through social media.

The expert quilting done on my Night and Day quilt was professionally longarm quilted by Mandy Leins of Mandaleiquilts.

Thank you Art Gallery Fabrics for supplying me with gorgeous fabrics to incorporate into my quilts. The quality of your material and incredible selection mixed seamlessly with my vintage stash.

ABOUT

Sharon has been quilting and sewing for over thirty years. Like her utility quilts, she brings practicability, beauty, and innovation to every aspect of her life, whether it's snapping a photograph, painting on canvas, or raising three children with her husband. After several successful business ventures and a full-time career as a mother, many winding roads collided to reconnect Sharon to her creative roots and love of fabric. She debuted her first of four fabric collections for Paintbrush Studios in 2011 and appeared in numerous quilting magazines. In 2012 she landed a career in the magazine industry as an assistant editor, graphic designer, and photographer for Quilt-it...Today! And Sew-it...Today! After more than two years as assistant editor Sharon felt it was time to find her artist's voice again. She joined Art Gallery Fabrics in 2014 with renewed vigor to design textiles and currently has five collections produced by Art Gallery Fabrics. Creating quilt patterns to share with quilters is a way for Sharon to share her love of the craft and infatuation with textiles.

NOTES